ISRAEL
A Colonial-Settler State?

Maxime Rodinson

ISRAEL

A Colonial-Settler State?

PATHFINDER

New York • London • Montreal • Sydney

Translated from the French by David Thorstad

ISBN 0-913460-23-0
Library of Congress Catalog Card Number 73-78187
Manufactured in the United States of America

First edition, 1973
Sixth printing, 1994

Cover: Palestinian refugees from the West Bank line up for a
United Nations ration distribution at the Damia Refugee Camp
in the East Jordan Valley following the 1967 war.

Pathfinder
410 West Street, New York, NY 10014, U.S.A.
Fax: (212) 727-0150 ▪ CompuServe: 73321,414
▪ Internet: pathfinder@igc.apc.org

Pathfinder distributors around the world:
Australia (and Asia and the Pacific):
    Pathfinder, 19 Terry St., Surry Hills, Sydney, N.S.W. 2010
    Postal address: P.O. Box K879, Haymarket, N.S.W. 2000
Britain (and Europe, Africa except South Africa, and Middle East):
    Pathfinder, 47 The Cut, London, SE1 8LL
Canada:
    Pathfinder, 4581 rue St-Denis, Montreal, Quebec, H2J 2L4
Iceland:
    Pathfinder, Klapparstíg 26, 2d floor, 101 Reykjavík
    Postal address: P. Box 233, 121 Reykjavík
New Zealand:
    Pathfinder, La Gonda Arcade, 203 Karangahape Road, Auckland
    Postal address: P.O. Box 8730, Auckland
Sweden:
    Pathfinder, Vikingagatan 10, S-113 42, Stockholm
United States (and Caribbean, Latin America, and South Africa):
    Pathfinder, 410 West Street, New York, NY 10014

Contents

Introduction

The aftermath of victory in war is usually rich in historical ironies, the unforeseen results that are quite the opposite of what the victors intended. One of the ironies of the third Arab-Israeli war is that this authoritative study of Israel's colonial-settler origins, by the French Jewish scholar, Maxime Rodinson, was just being set into type when Israel launched its blitz attack on the Arab forces in June 1967. For the results of that war were to give increased weight and credibility to Professor Rodinson's thesis which has long been heatedly denied by Zionist and Israeli leaders.

Maxime Rodinson, a director of studies at the Ecole Pratique des Hautes Etudes at the Sorbonne, is widely recognized as one of Europe's leading scholars in the field of Islamic and Middle Eastern studies. His essay first appeared in a special number of Jean-Paul Sartre's *Les Temps Modernes*, just as the war was ending. Entitled "*Le conflit israelo-arabe*," this special edition of nearly a thousand pages assembled contributions from leading Arab and Israeli intellectuals, mostly on the left, in an attempt at a "dialogue," dividing the articles into two sections, pro-Arab and pro-Israeli. Although Professor Rodinson's article is clearly sympathetic to the Palestinians, he preferred to have his article appear alone, apart from both ensembles, as a supplemental piece.

In a brief review in the *Middle East Journal*, Spring 1968, Prof. Irene Gendzier of Boston University called the special issue of Sartre's magazine a "unique document of extraordinary value" received in Paris with "the kind of welcome reserved for serious political-literary

events." However, in this country, she notes, it was subsequently "rejected for translation by several well-established American publishers on the unbelievable assumption
that the situation 'will soon be resolved.'" Professor Gendzier characterizes Rodinson's contribution as "by far the
most profound, if not the most controversial, summary
of the position that Israel is a colonial fact . . . the most
thorough and historically documented statement of [this]
position. . . ." She goes on to say that "its challenge has
already been felt, and the responses it is evoking among
Zionists and socialists alike can only serve to clarify
a historically complex and politically loaded subject."

The entire collection was forcefully brought to the attention of American left and liberal circles by the noted
journalist I. F. Stone, in a review article entitled, "Holy
War," in the August 3, 1967, *New York Review of Books*.
Stone considered Rodinson's contribution to be "by far
the most brilliant in the whole volume."

In that review, which aroused a storm of controversy,
Stone dismissed many of the standard Zionist arguments
as "simplistic sophistry." He decried the "moral myopia"
of Zionism which had always been blind to the national
existence of the Palestinian Arabs and the "moral schizo-
phrenia" involved in setting up an exclusionary and semi-
theocratic Jewish society when everywhere else Jewish survival counted on the maintenance of secular, pluralistic
societies.

For this and for his warm response to Professor Rodinson's analysis, Stone was denounced as a "defector" by
Zionists who formerly had praised him for his favorable
on-the-spot reports during the 1948 war to establish Israel.
They admitted the heavy blow dealt to their cause on
the plane of argument by a man with such credentials
for honesty and demonstrated sympathy for the Jewish
people.

Rodinson, too, has come in for his share of epithets,
which he wryly dismisses in one or two asides. A member of the French Communist Party for some twenty years
before he broke with it in 1958, Rodinson has a worldwide reputation as an independent Marxist scholar. Although it was not popular to do so, and even though

he disagreed sharply on many points, he lent his personal prestige to the work of a Belgian Trotskyist by writing the preface to the 1968 French edition of Abram Leon's *The Jewish Question, A Marxist Interpretation,*[1]* because he considered it an important intellectual and scientific contribution. While Rodinson belongs to no political party today, he has not withdrawn into an academic neutralism, but is involved and partisan in the contemporary social struggles.

On the other hand, he has nothing in common with the Communist Party academicians whose learned "findings" always serve to justify — and align their careers with — the latest turn in party policy, the Stalinist quotation jugglers who have done so much to discredit Marxism.

As readers will see, Rodinson takes great pains to develop a well-documented and thoughtful approach to the very specific, and central, question to which he limits himself in this study: Can Israel be classified as a colonial-settler state, and the Palestinians, concomitantly, as a people colonially oppressed by Israel? This is a major contention of the Arab side. But supporters of Israel, especially on the left, are outraged by such a characterization. They denounce it as pernicious propaganda, a slander and epithet directed by anti-Semitic reactionaries against a progressive and even socialist state established by a heroic people seeking to end thousands of years of exile and bondage.

Why is the same Middle Eastern reality viewed so differently by the two contenders? How is it possible to equate Israel with such odious colonial empires and white racist states as South Africa, Rhodesia, French Algeria?

The answer lies in rejecting any single model of colonial takeover, discarding rigidly conceived social formulas, and getting past the abstractions to the essential and concrete features of the complex, contradictory, and unique process which resulted in the creation of Israel.

Rodinson traces the origins and mentality of Zionism to the conditions of nineteenth and early twentieth century

---

*Notes begin on page 97.

Europe, when capitalism went through a period of great expansion and empire building which finally led to the first imperialist world war. Unfurling the banner of a universal (white) "civilizing mission," the European powers surged into the underdeveloped world, annexing colonial territories and mercilessly exploiting the subjugated peoples who were put to work on plantations and in mines to help in the looting of their own countries. But the Zionist nationalists, unlike other European colonialists, had to create a social base as well as take over a national territory.

The Jewish bourgeois and petty bourgeois strata which embraced Zionism were incomparably weaker than the European ruling classes and felt threatened by anti-Semitism, but they were just as fearful of socialist revolution. They were incapable of — and unwilling to — take up a national struggle claiming a section of Europe where the Jews lived, a struggle directed against their real oppressors that would have had revolutionary implications. Instead, a much more likely prospect was to find an empty, underdeveloped area — "a land without a people for a people without a land," as a leading Zionist publicist, Israel Zangwill, put it — upon which to settle those with nationalist aspirations. At the same time, this would drain off the excess of poor Jewish immigrants from Eastern Europe who were viewed by the well-to-do Jews as a causal factor in provoking anti-Semitism.

In common with the dominant outlook of European chauvinism, Zionism considered any territory as "empty" and available if its indigenous population had not yet achieved national independence and recognized statehood. Rodinson balances this harsh description of the early Zionists by pointing out that their racist prejudices and assumptions were no worse than those prevailing among their contemporaries, and might even be excused on that account as products of their time. This judgment can be questioned as overly charitable, in view of the existence — also among their contemporaries — of alternative movements for socialist and anti-imperialist liberation which were attracting far more of the Jewish youth than was Zionism. It certainly cannot excuse those who espoused this program in the name of socialism, either then or now. However, such considerations do not alter the basic facts.

Professor Rodinson demonstrates from the historical record and from numerous Zionist sources that Israel was established as the result of a colonial conquest, justified by an ethnocentric and racially exclusive ideology marked by the same chauvinist attitudes toward the peoples of underdeveloped lands as other European bourgeois nationalist doctrines. Complementing rather than challenging the delirious myths of anti-Semitism, the Zionist ideology basically accepted the fundamental tenet of the Jew as forever alien to "gentile" society, only affixing to this "eternal" characteristic a positive instead of a negative value.

Rodinson shows that plans for setting up an exclusively Jewish state in Arab Palestine got nowhere and found little favor even among Jews until British imperialism was persuaded to sponsor it in order to justify its own continued intervention in the Middle East. He proves that, despite its avowed humanitarian and liberationist aims, the Zionist project required the reciprocal collaboration of the Zionist agencies in upholding British rule against Arab strivings for independence, that it demanded the continued expansion of the bounds of Jewish settlement, the implantation of a modern economy and technology from which Arabs were excluded, and the ultimate displacement of the majority of the native Arab population from their own homeland.

Rodinson writes that among the Jews in Palestine during the mandate period, only a "few rare individuals" under the influence of "Stalinist ideology" opposed Zionism. It would appear that the opposition to Zionism by Jewish Stalinists rested on what remained of their grasp of Marxist internationalism, not on their Stalinist "ideology," which indeed permitted them to swing rapidly over to support the creation of Israel when that suited Stalin's foreign policy. The opposition to Zionism in Palestine should be extended, moreover, to include the small nucleus of Palestinian Trotskyists, Jewish and Arab, who functioned there since the 1930s. Their anti-Zionist positions, never compromised, have found vigorous new standard-bearers today among the young ranks of the Israeli Socialist Organization (Marxist), known as *Matzpen* (after their newspaper), who are under heavy attack today in Israel.

It is true that several hundred thousand Jews, fleeing Hitler before the war and escaping the wretched displaced persons camps after the war, found refuge in Palestine because they were not accepted by the western democracies who are today so friendly to Israel. These refugees, persecuted victims themselves, were absorbed into the settler community and only intensified the colonialist impact upon the Arabs. The same was true with the huge number of "Oriental" Jews who arrived afterwards — some under Zionist pressure and others expelled from their Arab countries of origin in stupid and reactionary "retaliation" for the expulsion of the Palestinians. In both cases, the Palestinians were made to suffer the consequences of the deeds of others.

That the Zionist state, once formed and well-established, could assume some of the more "normal" colonial relationships with the conquered people is becoming a source of deep concern and even embarrassment to some members of the Zionist establishment like Itzhak Ben-Aharon, the powerful secretary-general of the Histadrut labor federation. Terence Smith, Tel Aviv correspondent of the *New York Times*, reported on February 14, 1973, that Ben-Aharon raised the alarm "that six years of occupation had eroded Israel's image of 'moral capacity and reliability' in the Western world . . . he charged that Israel was 'building Zionism' on the backs of hired Arab labor from the occupied territory — a reference to the 55,000 Arab workers who have become the core of the manual labor force in Israel since the 1967 war." Ben-Aharon, who describes himself as a "radical Socialist," naturally does not ask that the 55,000 Arab laborers be given membership in the Histadrut and the protection it presumably affords Jewish workers. Instead, he demands that some of the occupied areas from which these workers come be returned to Jordan, much to the consternation of official Israeli opinion, which has become accustomed to holding these areas and to the presence of a cheap labor pool for the jobs that Jewish workers will no longer accept. Concern over these trends was well represented by a prominent Israeli dissident, Yehoshua Arieli, writing in the August 31, 1972, *New York Review of Books*, where he pointed to the effects of occupation in producing political conformity, spurring new vested interests, deepening social and material inequality, and leaving "Zionist values jettisoned" by hiring Arabs to do the dirty work.

This brings us back to the point made at the beginning, that the Israeli victory of 1967 produced a new situation which lent confirmation to Professor Rodinson's basic analysis. The new political dilemma was perceptively summarized by *New York Times* Jerusalem correspondent James Feron:

> The picture of an embattled state threatened by hostile neighbors has been blurred . . . with a picture of a victorious nation astride conquered lands and threatening disorganized neighbors. A new hero in the Middle East, the Arab guerrilla, has emerged since the war. The plight of the Arab refugees, largely forgotten by many after their first flight two decades ago, has become a live issue again. [2]

The dismaying new *social* dilemma confronting Israel was bluntly described by a leading Zionist functionary writing in the Israeli Labor Party daily, *Davar*, September 29, 1967. Joseph Weitz, former head of the Jewish Agency's Colonization Department, writes:

> . . . when the UN passed a resolution to partition Palestine into two states, the War of Independence broke out to our great good fortune; and in this war a twofold miracle happened: a territorial victory and the flight of the Arabs. In the Six Days' War one great miracle happened: a tremendous territorial victory; but most of the inhabitants of the liberated territories remained "stuck" to their places — which may destroy the very foundation of our state.

Weitz may define "liberation" differently than the Arab people who live in the "liberated territories," but nonetheless he put his finger on the great dilemma which the Zionist leadership thought it had evaded in 1948. Why was this "miracle" of the Arab flight, which Weitz elsewhere describes as equal to the miracle of Moses' crossing of the Red Sea, so necessary to Israel's survival? Weitz had long advocated a "transfer solution," miraculous or otherwise, to this dilemma. He explained why in an entry in his 1940 diary, which he quotes in his 1967 article:

> Between ourselves it must be clear that there is no room for both peoples together in this country . . . We shall not achieve our goal of being an independent people with the Arabs in this small country. The only solution is Palestine, at least Western Palestine [west of the Jordan River] without Arabs . . . And there is no other way but to transfer the Arabs from here to the neighboring countries; to transfer all of them; not one village, not one tribe should be left.

The support of other top Zionist figures like B. Katznelson and M. Ussishkin was secured at the time for this "solution," says Weitz, and "some preliminary preparations were made in order to put this theory into practice." No departure from Zionist attitudes was involved either, since the founder of the movement, Theodor Herzl himself, had proposed in his diary to "spirit" the Arabs across the border after denying them work in the Jewish state.

In 1948, the "transfer theory" was put into "practice," and largely failed to generate an outcry in the West. But in 1967, Israel clearly emerged from the war in the role of an annexationist, expansionist, and occupying power, ruling over vast new Arab territories and population masses who remained "stuck" to them. On the other hand, this outcome badly discredited all the Arab governments to whom the Palestinian refugees had looked for rescue. Israel thus promoted the very conditions for the growth of disillusionment at home and a shift in public opinion abroad, an increasing loss of faith in its democratic image and in the honor of its war aims, especially among the young. Simultaneously, it spurred the development of an independent and popular resistance movement among the Palestinians.

These resistance fighters put the entire struggle in a completely new light by raising the demand for Palestinian self-determination. They challenged the right of Israel to seize their homeland for exclusively Jewish use; they opposed the power of U. S.-backed Arab reactionaries like King Hussein; they rejected the "jihad" or holy-war demagogy designed to divert them from actual struggle and real liberation; and they proposed the establishment of a democratic secular Palestine for both Hebrew-speaking and Arabic-speaking peoples in the region. [3]

In addition to gaining the wide support of the Arab masses, the Palestinian struggle for self-determination has won the sympathy of many other people around the world, including American and Israeli Jewish youth influenced by the current radicalization affecting their generation and by the liberation struggles of other colonially oppressed nations like the Vietnamese. This has become a matter of deep concern for the Zionist coalition which runs Israel and has prompted renewed efforts by its "left" wing to win over radical-minded Jewish youth. This has, to be sure, always been the Zionist left's main political assignment.

However, their task is difficult because, from the beginning of the Zionist movement, there were always only two ways—either one equally hard to justify from a socialist standpoint—to achieve and maintain a Jewish state in Palestine, where the Arabs were a great majority. One was to expel the native Arabs, most of whom were not willing to give up their homeland and move away. The second was to institute a regime of occupation, with second-class citizenship rights, if any, for them. The 1947 UN partition resolution, under whose sanction Israel was established, scarcely altered this dual necessity, first because, in fact, there were still nearly as many Arabs as Jews in the portion assigned to Israel, and second, because the Zionist leadership always regarded that portion as merely the initial installment of the "redemption

of the historic homeland." Zionists will of course deny
their expansionist aims. But it is enough to ask almost
any Israeli leader if she or he would favor returning
all the territory seized in 1967 — in a war fought for "defensive purposes only" as Israel said then. The answer,
already given many times and in many forms, is no.

This is not only out of sentiment for the restoration of
the full extent of the ancient Hebrew kingdon. If land
seized in 1967 must be given back, then why not land
seized the same way in 1948? If the exclusive Jewish claim
to any part of Palestine can be challenged, then is the
claim to any other part secure?

That is why it is hard to see any possibility that the
"colonial situation" might have been "left behind" in 1948,
as Professor Rodinson suggests, if *two* states, Arab
Palestine and Israel, had emerged and been recognized
by the UN. The Israeli half of Palestine would certainly
still have remained the fruit of colonialism, and the whole
logic of the Zionist claim as well as the Arab resistance
to it would certainly not have been diverted by "com-
pensatory" UN recognition of a second arbitrarily created
Arab state. The only solution would have been for the
Palestinian Arabs to remove themselves voluntarily from
Israel in large numbers; and for those remaining to accept
a juridical double standard of immigration, settlement,
and civil laws — one for Jews, another for Arabs; in short
to voluntarily accept what no other people in history ever
freely accepted before! Strangely, until 1967, Israel and
its supporters seemed convinced that the Palestinians had
done just that!

It seems incredible that official Zionist and Israeli propaganda should still deny the historical reality, when
some of the Zionist chiefs themselves have occasionally
had to acknowledge it over the years, usually when baring
the facts of "practical" politics to troubled young people
in their ranks. It is even more incredible that the colonial-
settler character of Israel has not been widely recognized
by world public opinion, even among those who normally
sympathize with the colonially oppressed. This is not
due only to effective Zionist propaganda about the succour
of Jewish refugees, redemption of the sacred soil, or the

menace of Arab anti-Semitism. Nor was it due only to the universal guilt feelings after Hitler's abominations were revealed, which permitted the big powers to hand Palestine over to the Zionists in the name of atonement and compassion—and private relief that the Jewish survivors wouldn't be knocking at their doors.

No, it rests primarily on the fact that until 1967 the national existence of the Palestinian Arab people was simply denied. They were seen as unfortunate refugees, homeless largely by their own action, and at most in need of resettlement—when they were seen at all.

How did the Palestinians become so invisible? They outnumbered the Jews in Palestine eight to one in 1917, when the Balfour Declaration spoke of them as the "non-Jewish community" whose rights were not to be "prejudiced" by England's disposition of their territory. The Palestinians were still twice the Jewish population in 1948 when their territory was partitioned. To this day, if their scattered components living in the refugee camps, the occupied territories, and other Arab states were combined, they would still just about equal the Jewish population in Israel. How were they forgotten and made to disappear?

Many forces played a role in this great crime, beginning with the British imperialists and their Zionist proteges, who first stunted the economic and social development of the Arab community and then collaborated to crush its uprising in 1936-39, leaving it disorganized, disarmed, and helpless to resist in 1948. The pivotal character of this defeat was acknowledged by the military correspondent of the liberal Hebrew daily *Haaretz*, April 15, 1966:

> . . . with respect to the events of 1936, it seems to us that had they not happened in the manner and at the time in which they did in fact occur, it is doubtful that the Jewish community could have waged a war for independence eight years later. The Jewish community emerged from these dangerous 1936 events in a stronger position as a result of the strong support it received from the British government and army in Palestine.

The 1936 events actually involved a confrontation

between two national movements, but the Arabs made the mistake of concentrating their attacks on the British government and army . . . This confrontation with the British (and not with the Jews) caused the destruction of Arab military strength in Palestine, and was responsible for the partial elimination of Arab leadership in the country. After about three years of unequal warfare, Arab military power was destroyed; during this same period, however, the Jews, protected by the British, succeeded in building up their own strength . . . British reprisals against the Arab armed groups and against the Arab population were much more severe than those against Jewish clandestine organizations a few years later. [4]

The traditional Arab leadership, jealous of its own privileges, kept the resistance movement under its thumb, disoriented it politically, abandoned and betrayed it regularly. The imperialist powers ignored them as they ignored other peoples when carving up the world to suit their own interests. The UN lent its sanction to their dispersal. But the Palestinian people would not have become invisible, even after their defeat in 1948, had it not been for one crucial factor: betrayal by Stalin and the world's Communist parties. They enthusiastically championed the partition of Palestine after World War II. Stalin readily sacrificed the Palestinians' right to self-determination to the short-sighted diplomatic aim of easing British military power out of the Middle East where it had been entrenched since World War I. And when this plan, like so many others of Stalin's, backfired as Israel aligned itself with the more potent and threatening U.S. imperialism, the Kremlin courted not the disinherited Palestinians but the established Arab regimes, preferring maneuvers at the top to mobilization of a mass struggle.

The Kremlin placed the moral and political prestige of the Soviet Union, whose revolutionary origins and heroic victory over Nazism inspired the hopes of millions around the world for a socialist future, at the service of this unprincipled transaction, one of several such deals worked out with its imperialist wartime allies in Vietnam, Korea, Germany, and Eastern Europe. Designed to ensure "peaceful coexistence," those big power agreements proceeded without consideration for the interests and aspirations of the masses whose fate they were arbitrarily deciding. Only when these peoples rose up in revolutionary struggle to determine their own fate was their existence acknowledged. It can be safely concluded that, since the emergence of their resistance movement, the Palestinian Arab people will never again be invisible, whatever their temporary setbacks may be.

An important obstacle to the growth of a Jewish anti-Zionist movement among the young Israelis who already sympathize with the rights of the Palestinians, is the role of the "left" Zionist apologists for Israel. That is why one of the most valuable sections of Professor Rodinson's article, and one of the most effective, is his examination of the main Zionist rationalizations, from the religious to the "revolutionary," but especially the latter, in the light of the facts.

Kibbutz collectivism was far more important for settling new territory and guarding borders against dispossessed Arabs than for opening up a road to Jewish socialism. Moreover it involved only a small percentage of Jews — and of course no Arabs. The fight against the British was for exclusive control of the territory, not for the common liberation from imperialism for all those who lived there; nor did it give impetus or inspiration, as some contend, to the Arab independence struggle elsewhere. The argument that the region was originally barren and neglected is revealed to be a myth as well as a stock justification for colonial conquest, along with the argument that the Arabs remaining in Israel should be grateful for living better than their kin outside. The argument which attempts to find a scapegoat for Zionist outrages[5] in such openly chauvinist, right-wing extremists as Jabotinsky, Begin, and the Irgun terrorists, for whom the Zionist movement is held not to blame, is invalidated by the fact that all Zionists shared the fundamental goal of wresting Palestine from Arab hands and collaborated in this aim regardless of other differences. In this connection, Rodinson quotes the distinguished liberal Rabbi J. L. Magnes, who observed that the differences were diminishing and that "almost the entire movement has adopted Jabotinsky's point of view."

In the course of showing how the assertedly socialist outlook of the left Zionists, particularly of the early kibbutz settlers, failed to preserve them in the long run from the self-serving rationalizations of colonialism, Rodinson makes two generalizations in passing, and in a lengthy footnote, with which I would take issue.

First is that the attempted justification of Zionist positions against the Arabs largely stems from "the traditional line of thinking in European socialism that the only kind of relations a socialist society can possibly have with other societies are those motivated by the most deep-rooted altruism"; and that even the most socialist society internally could have relations with the outside world that denied the rights of other societies.

Second, that there is "a body of very general and very lasting psychological traits characterizing historic man" resulting from biological-social conditioning "since the beginning of human history (or at least since the neolithic revolution)" which has successfully resisted "the experiment of half a century of Soviet society with no private property in the means of production."

I shall not here go into the methodological correctness of putting the "collectivization" of the kibbutzim (which are in the historical line of utopian socialist colonies, such as New Harmony, or religious colonies, such as that of the Mormons in Utah) with the collectivization resulting from a social revolution. Nonetheless, I would agree with Rodinson that the argument that collectivization automatically makes for altruistic foreign relations on the part of a group or a state is a gross oversimplification of Marxism.

Collectivization can simply furnish the economic base for the production of such plenty that classes disappear and the individual need no longer scramble for material security and well-being; that consequently race and group antagonisms no longer have an internal base in the society and that, with the spread of similar systems internationally, the coercive functions of the state are no longer needed and atrophy.

But collectivization does not *ipso facto* automatically produce such fraternal relations internally or externally. The nationalized and planned economy in the Soviet Union proved strong enough to enable that society to industrialize and to withstand the second imperialist war but it failed to improve the conditions of life sufficiently for the transformation of the individual's psychology looked for by Rodinson. To cite the conditions of life in that period shows why: collectivization forced on the peasantry by massacres and mass deportations; poverty which made the peasant's private garden plot usually of greater value to him than his "share" of the collective farm's profit; instead of a period of security and plenty, an era of harsh deprivation and an undreamed of increase in coercion and fear. But the defects of the Soviet Union under Stalinism are not a proof of inherent defects of socialism; they merely underline the degree to which socialist norms have still to be attained in the Soviet Union.

Finally, on Rodinson's second point, it seems to me that if it is false to equate "collectivization" with "altruistic" attitudes in matters of foreign relations, it is equally erroneous to draw pessimistic conclusions about "human nature" because fifty years of Soviet collectivization failed to produce a society of altruistic individuals.

But what is the solution to the Arab-Israeli conflict? In a special section concluding his essay, Professor Rodinson ventures some opinions on this question. He doesn't believe there is a "revolutionary" solution and cautions against those who, safely distant from the scene of battle, "preach vengeance and murder from ivory towers." On the other hand, he appeals to readers on both sides to recognize the actual historical framework which, if it left the Zionists "no choice," as they claim, then it also left the Palestinians no choice but to resist and fight back. Rodinson himself calls for a "bloodless" solution and urges the Palestinians to avoid military methods, even though this may mean resigning themselves to their dispossession. But he rises above others who hold this position by insisting that it is up to the wronged party, namely the Arabs, to determine their goals and methods of struggle and that it is certainly impermissible for their oppressors to morally condemn the victims for the violence of their rebellion.

Professor Rodinson hopes that the passage of time may be able to assuage the deep and justified Arab resentment and permit the establishment of a *modus vivendi* based on the historical accomplished fact. To illustrate this variant, he cites the division of Ireland-Ulster which at the time of writing (1967) seemed to many observers to be working out. Today, of course, the turmoil in Ireland speaks powerfully against such expectations. The twenty years of patient, largely silent waiting by the Palestinian refugees, before they finally engaged in organized resistance, did not relieve their suffering nor prevent their blood from being spilled or their flesh from being seared by napalm. Their exile, unchallenged by active struggle on their part for so long, was thereby made more absolute, more difficult and costly to reverse.

Revolutionary supporters of the Palestinians do not, of course, "incite" them to violence. By far the greater violence involved in a struggle for national liberation comes from those upholding the status quo. A capable political leadership, unlike the desperate and misguided practioners of terrorist violence by a few martyrs, will know how to expose the real source of violence among the oppressors. It will know how to mobilize the Arab masses and world public opinion to hold back the unlimited violence that Israel, with its nuclear capacity and American military hardware, is prepared to unleash. A key factor in halting this violence will also be the development of a sizable revolutionary movement among Israeli Jews who reject Zionism and who see Jewish survival linked to a new socialist Palestine.

The Palestinian national liberation struggle is directed against the whole structure of privilege and exploitation, against both the Zionist and Arab ruling classes, as well as against imperialism. The Palestinian people have already demonstrated their capacity to play a vanguard role among the entire Arab people, but need time to develop an adequate revolutionary political leadership. Their immediate and pressing demand is for the dismantling of the Zionist state apparatus and the establishment of a democratic Palestine to restore their rights and their homeland. A revolutionary solution to the conflict envisions this accomplishment through the transformation of the whole region into a socialist society, the only kind of society that can redress the Palestinian grievances. At the same time, a socialist Palestine, as part of a socialist Middle East, would have plenty of room in it for a progressive Jewish community enjoying full democratic rights in language, culture, religion, employment, etc.; at peace with the Arabs; and playing its role in developing and advancing the area for the benefit of all who live there.

March 1973   PETER BUCH

What are the Arguments?

The theme of Judeo-Israeli colonialism plays a central role in the ideological controversy that usually accompanies, accelerates, amplifies and orchestrates the war — cold, hot, or lukewarm, depending on the period — between the Arabs and the Jewish-Palestinian *Yishuv** that has become the State of Israel. Confronting one another are strident assertions, sometimes worked out through aggressive theorizing. Can one attempt to make any sense out of it?

The accusation that Israel is a colonialist phenomenon is advanced by an almost unanimous Arab intelligentsia, whether on the right or the left. It is one case where Marxist theorizing has come forward with the clearest response to the requirements of the "implicit ideology" of the Third World, and has been most widely adopted.

On the other side, only the Israeli-Zionist left considers this charge slanderous. On the right it provokes only an uneasiness, more or less pronounced depending on how sensitive individuals and groups are to the spread of anticolonialist ideology on a world scale. It should be added that the theme has acquired an appreciable importance in the sphere of international political relations, in the diplomatic sphere. In the international forum provided by the United Nations, whether Israel is included in the camp of European imperialism or escapes this stigma makes a great deal of difference in relations with the Afro-Asian countries.

---

* *Yishuv*: Hebrew word for the Jewish community in Palestine at the time of the British Mandate — Ed.

It must be recalled that (as on many points) the present controversy at the state level was foreshadowed by theoretical, strategic, and tactical discussions within the Communist International. On yet another level, the first traces of it can also be found in the no less passionate controversies that have been going on for thousands of years between universalist Jews and nationalist Jews in the broadest sense of the terms.

Among the Arabs, there is certainly no dearth of assertions to choose from. Thus Nasser, in his *Philosophy of the Revolution*, relates his reflections as a 30-year-old officer returning from the Palestine war (1948-49):

> All this was in natural harmony with the view that experience had drawn in my mind. [The Arab East] comprised a single zone [in which were operating] the same circumstances and the same factors, and even all the same forces arrayed against it. It was obvious that imperialism was the most conspicuous of these forces. And Israel itself was nothing more than one of the consequences of imperialism. [1]

And here is the diagnosis of a Lebanese Communist just prior to the Palestine war:

> The Zionist movement is nothing but the exploitation, for the profit of Jewish capitalists linked to the aims of imperialism in the Arab East, of the feelings of a people that has gone through a great deal. . . . The Zionists have traded the unhappiness of their people for a commercial undertaking and a colonialist platform. [2]

Subsequent years have only impelled the Arab revolutionary forces to expand upon this analysis by linking Zionism to the worldwide system of imperialism. The draft national charter presented by President Gamal Abdel Nasser to the National Congress of Popular Forces in Egypt on May 21, 1962, states:

The determination of our people to put an end to the hostile conduct of Israel on a portion of the Palestinian fatherland is equivalent to a decision to liquidate one of the most dangerous pockets of the battle being waged by imperialism against the peoples' struggle. And our consistent policy of going after Israeli infiltration in Africa is nothing but an attempt to limit the spread of a deadly imperialist cancer. [3]

This concept of Israel as a multi-tentacled imperialist agent was especially developed with regard to its infiltration into Africa, for example, by Mehdi ben Barka at the World Conference on Palestine held in Cairo March 30-April 6, 1965. [4]

Thus, for the Arabs, Israel is an imperialist base set up in the Middle East by British imperialism in collusion with others; it is part of a worldwide imperialist system; and therefore the activity it carries on throughout the world, whether on its own behalf or on behalf of American and European imperialism, is of an imperialist nature. This at least is the most common view; and while it comes out of left-wing circles, it is accepted on a much broader scale. Naturally, this view is accepted or assimilated with many nuances. [5] At the very least, there is the feeling of having undergone a humiliation inflicted by a foreign element supported by powerful forces in the European-American world.

Naturally, Zionist and pro-Israeli writers have applied themselves to refuting these accusations.

Thus, these writers stress the socialist character of the Zionist movement. Sweeping Herzl and the official Zionist Organization under the rug as much as possible, they emphasize everything in the present Israeli situation that derives from socialist ideologies. They stress the importance of the influence of the Marxist Zionist Ber Borochov (1881-1917), who stood up to the Zionist Organization, interpreting Jewish history in terms of class struggles and glorifying the Jewish proletariat, whose victory could only become a reality in Palestine. Along with this current, the thought of Aaron David Gordon (1856-1922), a socialist of Tolstoyan inspiration who praised the value of work and who spent the last part of his life in the Degania kibbutz, is brought forward. The ideas of these socialist thinkers, whether Marxists or not, are presented as having become embodied in powerful movements that contributed greatly to orienting the waves of Jewish emigrants in Palestine and their constructive work. Naturally, Israel's more or less collectivist colonies, and the institutions that have developed around the network they form, are considered, correctly, to be the concrete products of this ideological movement, and are presented as models of socialist accomplishment. The implicit conclusion is that a society so deeply permeated with the leaven of socialism cannot be termed colonialist or imperialist.

In order even further to emphasize this characterization of Israel as socialist, the Arab world is portrayed as being feudal at the outset, and today partly fascist. Contrary to the Arab conception, therefore, the struggle between the two societies is seen as that of a progressive, socialist, revolutionary force against the bulwarks of social backwardness or reaction. One of the most extreme representatives of this view has been Abdel-Razak Abdel-Kader (a descendant of the great Algerian emir), an Arab who converted to Zionism and whose work, published by Francois Maspero, has been enthusiastically greeted by the French left. [6]

According to some, the State of Israel, far from being the result of any imperialist wave, was established in the course of a struggle against British imperialism. It is this struggle, and not the struggle of the Arabs for independence, that is part of the great liberation movement of our epoch. It is even said to be responsible for giving the initial impetus to the Arab movement.

"Through the withdrawal of British troops from Palestine and the proclamation of an independent Jewish state," wrote Robert Misrahi on this very point, the new Israelis ". . . ushered in a genuine liberation movement that was to become as much their own history as that of the Mediterranean Arabs. If the English had remained in Palestine, they would never have left Egypt, and if

Glubb Pasha had conquered the Israelis in 1948, he would never have been chased out of Jordan."[7] Besides, many add, this independence was obtained with the help of the socialist countries. Czech weapons played a role in it, a speech by Gromyko to the UN (often quoted) was the prelude to the transformation of a part of Palestine into a Jewish state, and the USSR was the first to recognize this state.

The difference with the usual criteria used to define colonialism is also stressed. In reply to my remarks at the Mutualite on March 5, 1964, the Union of Jewish Students in France (UEJF) wrote:

> Not one of the traits that characterize colonialism — the military lending a strong hand to missionaries in order to open up a path for merchants and to make it possible to exploit the labor of the colonized — can be found in the Jewish immigration movement in Palestine. In place of a mother country — Jews chased from one country to another in Europe; in place of soldiers — proletarians and intellectuals armed with pickaxes; merchants (Jews=merchants?) — there were none; as for missionaries, it would be well to recall that Zionism was a lay movement inspired by socialism (for example, Borochov).[8]

Finally, added to these arguments dealing mainly with the inspiration and origin of the Zionist movement and the State of Israel are reflections concerning the internal relations of the Jewish immigrants with the country's Arabs. The purchase of Arab land that provided a foundation for the Jewish state was not at all an act of plunder, according to Robert Misrahi, who develops this theme at length.[9] On the level of ethics in general, it could be said "with Rousseau and Marx that the land belongs to those who cultivate it." (p. 2186) But, more concretely, and in contrast to the case of Algeria, where "when the French arrived, all the good land was cultivated by the Algerians, in Palestine the Jewish immigrants found only uncultivated land and deserts." (p. 2190) The Arabs, moreover, could be forgiven for not having cultivated their land. They had been "feudalized" for four centuries by the Turks and exploited by them in colonial style. (p. 2194) "Most of the land that was sold belonged to big absentee landlords," whether "Turkish landlords residing in Turkey or in Syria" or "feudal Arab magnates, for the most part Syrian" (p. 2203), and therefore absent from the country. "To be sure, there were also small Arab landholders who sold their land to the Jews." But, "weighed down by taxes, tenures, or rents," with no "prospect of gain" on collective land divided into lots that were redistributed every two years, [10] only the money they received from selling could make it possible for them to develop their methods a little (p. 2204). The purchased land, which was paid for at a very high price, was only a fraction of the arable land (so there was some, after all!) and thus by no means involved a general dispossession of the Arabs.

The UEJF states: "The essential and original characteristic of Palestinian Jewish society before 1948 was to not depend in any way upon the exploitation of the labor of the Arab fellow countrymen. On the contrary, the improvement of the country was accomplished through the manual labor of Jewish cooperative laborers and *kibbutznikim* [members of a *kibbutz*, or collective farm — Editor]. Where, then, is the colonialism?" And R. Misrahi stresses the conditions under which the Keren Kayemet Le-Yisrael (Jewish National Fund or JNF) cedes back its lands. "The temporary tenant will, under any and all circumstances, have to work his land himself and not have it worked by others, whether Jews or Arabs. By a detour through Biblical mythology, one thus arrives at the revolutionary result of banning exploitation of the labor of others" (p. 2201), at least on the lands of the JNF (300,000 hectares out of 800,000 presently arable) [hectare = 2.47 acres — Editor]. [11]

Thus the Arab Palestinian *fellahin* [peasants] are not exploited. And by the very fact that the Jews have settled there, their standard of living, their buying power, and their cultural, technical and health standards have been raised to a considerably higher level, so that they are now much better off in Israel in every respect than they would be in the independent Arab countries. The image they present seems to have little in common with that of miserable victims of colonialism.

In What Way is Israel a Colonial Phenomenon?

The entire angry polemic of the Zionists and the pro-Israelis against the image that the Arabs as well as a certain number of Marxists have of Israel is, indeed, inspired by very powerful psychological stereotypes. The victim of colonization is the starving wretch in rags, his eyes filled with fear, trapped and miserable, searching anxiously for a scrap of food. The colonizer is the military or civilian brute, either arrogantly toying with his cane, flaunting himself in a rickshaw pulled by worn-out coolies, or else, half-drunk and insensate, raping little black girls. How is it possible to fit into this picture either these noble Israeli Arabs whom government publications show solemnly placing their votes in a democratic ballot box or seriously taking part in the deliberations of some municipal council, or the *kibbutznik* with his pure face, aglow with idealism, working with his hands on the very land Solomon, Isaiah and Jesus trod, having overcome and left behind the scars of forebears degraded by ghetto life?[12] All the rest is only the rationalization of an indignant rejection of the possibility that these sharply contrasting images — all of which, moreover, contain their element of truth — can be reconciled.

This refusal is understandable. But an attempt must be made to investigate the problem a little more seriously. The UEJF text mentioned above retains traces of an effort to be more rigorous. But, so often, attempts in this vein slide almost fatally into the kind of concern for "realism" in the scholastic sense of the term that feeds so many "metaphysical" visions of concrete reality. Some argue as though colonialism were a creation of the mind, an immediately recognizable entity, clearly demarcated from right to left and top to bottom, and identifiable by some unambiguous definition as a plant or animal is. This is a common practice that seems impossible to uproot and that continues to wreak havoc in the social sciences and the ideologies in which they bask.

There is no such thing as colonialism and imperialism as such. What there is is a series of social phenomena in which numerous analogies with one another can be found, but also infinite nuances, and which have come to be referred to with labels. There is a central core, so to speak, on which everyone agrees, but which imperceptibly tapers off at the outer edges into a region where terminology varies according to groups, schools of thought, and even individuals. Hence the differing dictionary definitions.

On the other hand, Zionism is an ideological movement of vast scope which has acquired a history that is already old and for which percursors can still be found. It has always taken many forms and has encompassed numerous divergent tendencies, as can be seen from even the slightest glance at its tormented and tumultuous history, at the schisms and splits it has produced, and at the fierce internal struggles that have marked it. In addition, as with any ideological movement, one must differentiate between ideal principles and variants that crop up in internal tendencies and with the passage of time, the implicit or explicit motivations of the masses of followers, the strategic and tactical plans of the leaders, the fulfillment of these plans (which is always only partial and which always comes about in somewhat unforeseeable circumstances), the consequences of these plans, etc. All this would involve numerous nuances that I am afraid could be dealt with here only very inadequately.

Yet overall characterizations are possible. It cannot be denied that the motivations of the masses who gave the Zionist movement its strength had little in common with those of the British capitalists, whose imperialist ambitions were given theoretical shape by Joseph Chamberlain. These masses were essentially moved by deep disgust with the oppressive conditions they had been subjected to in Czarist Russia and in Eastern Europe in general. Their revolt (as justifiable as any other revolt) against these conditions was channeled into various paths depending on the groups and individuals involved, and in line with their particular situation and history. The influence of already existing ideologies (though it varied from case to case) played a key role.

In the face of the humiliating situation confronting them, certain assimilated Jews chose political and, occasionally, revolutionary struggle in the countries they felt themselves to be citizens of, side by side with non-Jews of the same persuasion, in the midst of a people they wanted to be a part of. Others, like the Bundists,* engaged in similar struggles, but in groups made up entirely of Jews. Still others rejected any link with the people, country and state into which they had been integrated and placed their hope in another homeland, a purely Jewish homeland. Many were quite indifferent as to the actual location of this homeland. In 1904, a French Jew who was making inquiries at Berdichev noted that the local Jews were not concerned about whether or not he and his companions were Zionists. More than anything else, they wanted to know if they were not delegates from the Jewish Colonization Association which was setting up Jewish agricultural colonies almost everywhere, especially in America. "Indeed, Palestine is less attractive to them than emigration."[13] Yet several factors were to give Palestine special preference in the dreams of the future.

The location of the Jewish homeland was not the least bit in doubt for those who remained tied to the ancestral religion providing they had rejected religious objections against carrying out divine plans with purely temporal means. The entire Jewish tradition, kept alive from generation to generation through reading and studying the sacred texts and their commentaries, through prayers

---

Members of the Bund: the "General Jewish Workers Union of Lithuania, Poland, and Russia;" an important Jewish socialist, anti-Zionist organization founded in 1897 and destroyed during World War II — Ed.

and in all of the literature, named Palestine, in the circumlocution of Deuteronomy, "the land which the Lord your God giveth you to inherit"; this country that till the end of time was to be the site of the Messianic reign of happiness and joy, in the shadow of the city of Jerusalem, "the city of the Great King," where, at the end of each Passover meal, one expresses the hope of finding oneself the following year. Many of those who were moving away in varying degrees from the ancestral religion (with the usual inconsistency of waning ideologies) retained intact the attachment for this country that had been passed down by such a persistent cultural tradition. The nationalist orientation of the movement could not help but favor an ideological development in which the one historically certified homeland of the Jews as Jews would play a central role. Even socialists, whether Marxist or Tolstoyan, quite naturally adopted this choice of location once they chose to orient toward a regroupment of Jews in a new homeland. A purely Jewish socialist society would have to be located somewhere and what better region to shelter it in than the one indicated by all of Jewish history?

There was not necessarily any colonialist or imperialist orientation per se in the motivations underlying this choice. The element that made it possible to connect these aspirations of Jewish shopkeepers, peddlers, craftsmen, and intellectuals in Russia and elsewhere to the conceptual orbit of imperialism was one small detail that seemed to be of no importance: Palestine was inhabited by another people. It would be very interesting to go through newspapers and books to see what kind of ideas the Jewish masses of Eastern Europe had about the indigenous populations in Palestine. They must have been very vague, bearing only a remote resemblance to reality. Besides, in terms of the ideals whose realization was seen occurring in some far off future, the "Palestinophilia" of the Russian Jew, as it was called, lacked any clearly defined political goal, and consequently did not even deal with the question.

This "Palestinophilia" or Jewish counterreaction to the wave of anti-Semitism unleashed in 1881, which Simon Dubnow calls the "second reaction," [14] was based on simple ideas. "Lilienblum, Pinsker, Lewanda," writes this learned historian (an anti-Zionist Jewish nationalist), "out of disappointment in their hope of civil emancipation, proclaimed the slogan: 'We are strangers everywhere, we must return home!' This simple, elementary response to the complex national question became an alluring theory for many, but in practice bore only limited results. The great masses of emigrants could not find room enough for themselves on the narrow path of Palestinian colonization foreseen by the pioneers and enthusiasts of the idea. The annual emigration of several hundred men to Palestine, at a time when tens of thousands were leaving for America, made hopes of transplanting the core of the Jewish people from the Diaspora to the historical homeland appear groundless."[15]

In the period of hoping, one either held onto one's religious belief and placed confidence in God to mysteriously convert the presence of a few scattered pioneers into a Messianic kingdom, or one put off the problem into an indefinite future. Any thought about the country's current inhabitants scarcely disturbed what were vague ideas based only on problems relating to Judaism or Jewishness. Only a few lucid minds (among them the theoretician of "spiritual Zionism," Ahad Ha'am, as early as 1891) drew attention to the fact that Palestine was not an empty territory and that this posed problems.[16] They hardly met with any response at all. A quite excusable and understandable indifference, but one that bore within it the seed of future conflicts. Moreover, it was an indifference linked to European supremacy, which benefited even Europe's proletarians and oppressed minorities. In fact, there can be no doubt that if the ancestral homeland had been occupied by one of the well-established industrialized nations that ruled the world at the time, one that had thoroughly settled down in a territory it had infused with a powerful national consciousness, then the problem of displacing German, French, or English inhabitants and introducing a new, nationally coherent element into the middle of their homeland would have been in the forefront of the consciousness of even the most ignorant and destitute Zionists.

But European supremacy had planted in the minds

of even the most deprived of those who shared in it the idea that any territory outside Europe was open to European occupation. From this point of view the Zionist brand of utopia was essentially no different from socialist utopias like Cabet's Icaria. It was a matter of finding an empty territory — empty not necessarily in the sense of actual absence of inhabitants, but rather of a kind of cultural barrenness. Outside the boundaries of civilization, as Metternich said, European "colonies" could be freely placed not in opposition to but in the midst of more or less backward peoples; these "colonies" could not help but become poles of development, to use a recent term anachronistically. The Ottoman Empire to which Palestine belonged seemed at the very least to be covered with culturally barren spots.

This stands out most clearly in the developmental stage of the theory, in the works of the theoretical founders of political Zionism. Leo Pinsker (1831-1891), an assimilationist who was converted to Jewish nationalism by the pogroms of 1881, noted the turning of Russian and Rumanian Jews toward Palestine in the wake of this martyrdom. "However much in error this turn might have been . . . it is no less a testimony to their just instincts as a people: they realize they must have their own homeland."[17] The basic aspiration was just, but the focus of the Jewish hopes was a little gratuitous, he thought. "We cannot dream about restoring ancient Judea. It would no longer be possible for us to begin anew there where once our political life was brutally interrupted and destroyed. . . . The goal of our efforts must not be the *Holy* Land, but a Land *Of Our Own*. All we need is a large territory for our ill-fated brothers, a territory that remains our own property and from which no foreign master can chase us. . . . It is even possible that the Holy Land will again become our country. So much the better. But the most important thing is to determine quite simply which country is open to us. . . ."[18]

The country had to be selected above all on the basis of the objective advantages it offered. "The territory that we are to acquire must be fertile, favorably located, and large enough to accommodate several million men. . . .

The choice could be made between a small territory in North America or a soverign *pashalik** whose neutrality would be guaranteed as much by the Porte** as by other powers."[19] A committee of experts would decide. It will perhaps opt for Palestine or Syria if it is possible "to make the country very productive within a certain length of time." If it opts for America, it will have to hurry because "today the acquisition of vast domains in America is not too risky an undertaking," but the population of the United States is growing very quickly. However, all this is of secondary importance compared to the "self-emancipation of the Jewish people as a nation, through the creation of a Jewish *colonial* community destined one day to become our inalienable, inviolable homeland — our own homeland [emphasis added]."[20] The objection to all this was certainly foreseen, but not in terms of the rights of the people in whose midst they were to settle, but rather in terms of a collision between political powers: "What country will permit us to set ourselves up as a nation within the confines of its territory?" Well, the governments that have persecuted us will help us, for they "will no doubt take as much pleasure in seeing us leave as we will in leaving." And "it is obvious that the creation of a Jewish home could never happen without the support of governments."[21]

Things were seen no differently fourteen years after Pinsker's manifesto in the other great manifesto — the one that got the Zionist movement proper going — *The Jewish State* by Herzl (another assimilated Jew who converted). And the convergence in the ideas of these two authors who did not know each other is significant. "Two territories are under consideration: Palestine and Argentina. Experiments in Jewish colonization worth noting have taken place on these two points. . . . Should preference be given to Palestine or Argentina? The Society [the "Society of Jews" which Herzl proposed be founded to repre-

---

**Pashalik:* Ottoman administrative district governed by a pasha — Ed.

***Porte:* the Ottoman government — Ed.

sent all Jews who supported the idea of a Jewish state—MR] will take what it is offered, taking into account indications of Jewish public opinion regarding it. It will look into both. Argentina is one of the richest countries of the world in natural resources, colossal in size and with a small population and a temperate climate. It would be of great interest to the Argentine republic to grant us a piece of its territory . . . Palestine is our unforgettable historical homeland. Its name alone would be a powerfully stirring rallying cry for our people."[22]

Thus, due to the very fact that they specified the ultimate goal in terms of a Jewish state, the theoreticians naturally had to be much more concerned than the masses, in their confused aspirations, were with the location of the country to be occupied and the attitude of the governments and peoples concerned toward their demands. Pinsker, who was less realistic, was satisfied to hope that the shores they reached would be less inhospitable than the countries they left, and that the governments of these countries (especially Russia) would help with the migration. Herzl had a better grasp of the concrete problems. But if, beginning with his manifesto, he was exceedingly preoccupied with governments and their attitude, he viewed the public opinion of the peoples affected as nothing more than a collection of prejudices that would have to be defused and combatted.

Both his approach and that of the organization he created were approaches that unquestionably fit into the great movement of European expansion in the nineteenth and twentieth centuries, the great European imperialist groundswell. There is no reason whatsoever to be surprised or even indignant at this. Except for a section (only a section) of the European socialist parties and a few rare revolutionary and liberal elements, colonization at the time was essentially taken to mean the spreading of progress, civilization and well-being.

The world at that time was dominated by the great European imperialist powers. Any undertaking aiming to bring about a political transformation would have to obtain at least their consent, and better yet, their support. For this, it would have to offer advantages for these powers and fit into their plans. And that was a consideration that any realistic mind would have to take into account. Around the same period, the father of Moslem nationalism, Jamal ad-din al-Afghani, was spending his life, like Herzl, sounding out which powers might back his plans, attempting to play off one against the other.

Pinsker, as we have seen, had already been aware of the need for this policy. Herzl was very clear about it. It is in fact on this point that he polemicized against Zionists who preceded him, against what was sometimes called *hovevei-zionism*, [23] and implicitly also against the "spiritual Zionism" of Ahad Ha'am, [24] who wanted only to form a "spiritual center" in Palestine around which the ideal unity of the scattered Jewish nation could crystallize. Scattered agricultural colonies struck Herzl as ineffectual. They are based on "the false principle of successive infiltration." But, "infiltration must always end badly because, without fail, the moment comes when the government, on the urging of the populations who feel they are threatened, stops the influx of Jews from the outside. As a result, immigration is only truly viable if it is based on assurances of our sovereignty. The Society of Jews will negotiate with the sovereign authorities of the territories in question, and it will do so under the protectorate of the European powers, if they find the arrangement to their liking." [25]

And Herzl attempted to portray the advantages the new state could hold in store for those who ceded territory for it and for those powers who helped bring about this transfer of land. Here is what he foresaw, should Palestine be the territory selected:

> If His Majesty the Sultan were to give us Palestine, we could undertake to regulate Turkey's finances. For Europe, we would constitute a bulwark against Asia down there, we would be the advance post of civilization against barbarism. As a neutral state, we would remain in constant touch with all of Europe, which would guarantee our existence. [26]

It would have been difficult to place Zionism any more clearly within the framework of European imperialist policies. This was indeed the path followed by the Zionist Organization, founded by Herzl at the Congress of Basel in August 1897. The program adopted at Basel defined the goal of Zionism as "the creation in Palestine of a homeland for the Jewish people guaranteed by public law (*die Schaffung einer oeffentlich-rechtlich gesicherten Heimstaette in Palaestina*)." The term "guaranteed by public law" had been hotly debated. "Guaranteed by public law" (from the text of the initial plan) appeared too vague, and "guaranteed by international public law (*voelkerrechtlich gesicherte*)"[27] too restrictive. In the thinking of the founders, the text that was adopted meant: to seek autonomy for a Jewish Palestine under the sovereignty of the sultan and with the guarantee of the great powers. Christian Lebanon provided a precedent. A pact or charter guaranteed by the great powers was to set down the respective rights and duties of the Ottoman sovereign and the Jewish colonists. The underlying desire for a completely independent Jewish state was not expressed, though it was certainly there in the background. Besides, this was a time when territories within the Ottoman Empire that were inhabited by other peoples were being granted independence one after the other. Why should the future Jewish territory be any exception?

The four points of the Basel program flowed in the most logical fashion from such an ultimate goal: the development of craft and agricultural colonization in Palestine, an effort to organize the scattered Jewish people, an effort to increase their "national consciousness," and last but not least, the undertaking of preliminary steps to obtain the necessary governmental agreements.

Everyone could see that once the goal was a Jewish state, and not scattered colonies or a purely spiritual center, the support of the great powers would be necessary. First of all directly, so that the pact with the Ottoman sultan, who for the time being had sovereignty over Palestine, would enjoy international guarantees against the dangers of any attempt to renege on it (the massacres of Armenians gave some idea of the catastrophic consequences such an attempt could lead to). And then also indirectly, to pressure the sultan, if he proved stubborn, into allowing free immigration, or more fundamentally, into granting autonomy. In all these eventualities, the perspective was inevitably placed within the framework of the European assault on the Ottoman Empire, this "sick man" whose complete dismemberment was postponed by the rivalries of the great powers but who, in the meantime, was subjected to all kinds of interference, pressures, and threats. An imperialist setting if there ever was one.

This search for the indispensable backing of the great powers inescapably dictated Zionist policy toward them — to play upon their rivalries; to pressure them to the extent that this was made possible by the electoral or financial power of their Jewish populations, even when the latter had been only theoretically won to Zionism; or, on the other hand, to play on their anti-Semitism and their desire to get rid of the Jews. It was in this spirit that in 1903 Herzl reached a general agreement on fundamentals with the sinister Plehve, Czarist minister of the interior and organizer of pogroms,[28] inaugurating a political tradition of converging the Zionist program with that of the anti-Semites (something Herzl proudly admitted), [29] and which was to be almost fatal.[30]

Every revisionist political plan had to follow this kind of policy, and as we have already seen, this was also the policy of various nationalist tendencies in the Moslem world, in the early stages of Egyptian and Arab nationalism in particular. But Zionist Jewish nationalism had the advantage of being able to count on more or less powerful support among citizens of the imperialist states themselves and to draw upon a mass base in Eastern Europe. The Europeanism of the Zionists made it possible for them to present their plan as part of the same movement of European expansion that each power was developing on its own behalf. Hence, the many statements pointing out that it was in the general interest of Europe or civilization (which amounted to the same thing), or even in the particular interest of this or that power, to support the Zionist movement. This was perfectly natural given the atmosphere of the period. There is no need for us to moralize by applying to the Zionist leaders or masses of that time criteria that have become common today. But neither do we have the right to deny that their attitude was what it was, nor to disregard its objective consequences.

It was within this perspective that the Zionist plan was presented. It is within this perspective that it became a reality. This was made possible by a British political charter, the Balfour Declaration of November 2, 1917, which informed Lord Rothschild that "His Majesty's government view with favour the establishment in Palestine of a national home for the Jewish people. . . ." What were the motives of the British government, and what was the respective weight of each? This is a difficult historical problem to resolve in detail with great accuracy, but the general outline of such a solution is rather easy to perceive.[31] Let us, along with the Arab historian George Antonius, moreover, discard the stale anti-Semitic theories that would have the declaration be payment in return for the alleged efforts of American Jews to draw the United States into World War I, or even the large-scale purchase of war bonds by British Jews (actually, those Jews who bought the most were anti-Zionist). We must also discard the romantic theory that claimed it was a reward to the Zionist leader Chaim Weizmann for inventing a powerful explosive! On the other hand, one cannot accept this same Weizmann's thesis that the declaration was above all a "unique act of the world conscience"[32] helped more than anything else by the alluring appeal the great Zionist Return held out for British souls brought up on the Bible.[33] Certainly this feeling played some role in the background. But the cabinet of a nation involved in a hazardous and difficult world war does not decide to take actions of such scope on the basis of such feelings. Actually, Weizmann knew this very well, for having been warned that the anti-Zionist Jewish minister Edwin Montagu[34] was going to violently oppose the declaration at a discussion of the problem by the War Cabinet, he made sure the cabinet received a note containing these words: ". . . in submitting our resolution we entrusted *our national and Zionist destiny to the Foreign Office and the Imperial War Cabinet* in the hope that the problem would be considered in the light of imperial interests and the principles for which the Entente stands."[35] [Emphasis in the original — Editor].

The great motives behind the declaration lie in the desired propagandistic impact on the Jews of the Central Empires and Russia, and the hope of developing a claim in the future liquidation of the Ottoman Empire. The Jews of Germany (where the offices of the Zionist Organization were located until 1914) and of Austria-Hungary had been won to the war effort largely because it involved fighting Czarist Russia, persecutor of the Jews. In conquered Russian territory, the Germans had given the appearance of being protectors of the oppressed Jews and their liberators "from the Muscovite yoke."[36] The Russian Revolution reinforced defeatist tendencies inside Russia. An important role in the Russian revolutionary movement was attributed to Jews. It was crucial to give them reasons to support the allied cause. It is by no means coincidental that the Balfour Declaration preceded by five days the fateful date of November 7 (October 25 on the Julian calendar) when the Bolsheviks took power. One of the aims of the declaration was to support Kerensky. Thought was also given to the weight of the Jews in the United States, a country that had just joined forces with the Allies. A maximum effort on its part was needed at a time when it was more inclined toward pacifism.[37] The German and Austrian Zionists, who were carrying on negotiations with their governments to obtain a kind of "Balfour Declaration" from the Turkish government,[38] had to be brought along. As far as Palestine was concerned, it was not a bad prospect for England to have at its disposal in the Near East a population tied to it both by recognition and need at a time when the agreement of the Sharif of Mecca, Hussein, to mount a revolt against the Turks had been obtained by promising him a large Arab kingdom; when the secret Sykes-Picot agreement (at the beginning of 1916) had divided up this same region into zones of influence between England and France; and when the latter was using its Lebanese contacts especially to lay plans for a greater Syria (including Palestine) under French influence.[39] To make a special question out of Palestine, and to grant Great Britain a particular responsibility for it, was to provide itself with a solid basis for making demands during the partition that would follow the war. Weizmann insists that it was he and his staff who first asked the reticent English to assume a protectorate role over the future Jewish state.[40] Perhaps. But, the suggestion ended up being very favorably received. And the big obstacle was France, which, through Georges Picot, was laying claim to this protectorate over Palestine if a Jewish state were created.[41]

The Balfour Declaration, which was a British political act, could only be applied in the wake of a successful military undertaking attributable essentially to Great Britain, backed up by France and the United States: victory over the Ottoman Empire in Palestine and Syria[42] at the end of 1917 and in 1918. At that point, the most concrete political problems were raised. Until then, as Weizmann says, the Arab question had not been in the foreground and the Zionists had in fact ignored it.[43] Now it became crucial. All of a sudden, the Arabs became an important element in the political game.

Several decades earlier it might have been possible to carry through the Zionist plan on the level the political Zionists envisaged through deals between a Zionist Organization, endowed with great resources, and governments, essentially those of the European imperialist powers. Unfortunately for them, the stage for putting this plan into effect arrived at a time when nationalism was taking shape in the Moslem countries too. In Sultan Abdul Hamid, the Zionist leaders had run into the reticence of a landlord who saw that his Empire might once again be carved up.[44] They had run into religious resistance among his entourage, and they had met with the very justified fear of the Ottoman government that the introduction of a new "national" element into the heart of the Empire would end, as it had in Greece, Bulgaria, Rumania, and Serbia, with demands for independence supported from outside, and in new and fatal wars for the Empire. This very perceptive analysis finally led the sultan to decide to turn down offers from Herzl that seem to have strongly appealed to him from a financial point of view, [45] but which he used primarily as a way of getting other no less disinterested parties to increase their offers to help restore the Ottoman finances. [46]

The quite recent remarkable study by Neville Mandel, [47] which is based on the best sources, demonstrates that, contrary to the prevailing opinion up to now, Arab resistance to Zionist colonization in Palestine began as soon as this colonization got under way, well before the war of 1914-1918. But at first it was not political. The peasants opposed the Zionist colonies to the degree that they collided with their interests; then they resigned themselves and set up a modus vivendi with them that was sometimes to their own advantage. If the big landholders rejoiced at the jump in the price of land, and if the masses remained indifferent, in the cities the merchants and all those belonging to what we would call the service industry (a layer made up mostly of Christians) protested, fearing eventual economic competition. The stir made by Herzl's book in 1896, the first Zionist political congress in 1897, and the steps Herzl had taken with the sultan began to give a boost to the opposition, but the Ottoman government's hostility to Zionism seemed assurance that the danger remained very remote. Arab nationalism, which was developing with difficulty in opposition to the Turks, and which, in the beginning, attracted Christians especially, began to show through in protests against Zionist colonization only after 1905. The Young Turk Revolution of 1908, which granted freedom of political expression and permitted the formation of parties, made it possible for groups to articulate diffuse feelings of discontent, to draw appropriate conclusions in programs and to try to mobilize the masses around them. From another angle, the policy of Turkization that quickly became the policy of the group in power, the Union and Progress Committee, contributed heavily toward hardening the positions of the Arabs and pushing the Moslems toward Arab nationalism. Arab members of the Ottoman parliament brought up the question of Zionism there. The shape of things on the political level still greatly complicated the picture. On the one hand the Union and Progress Committee maintained restrictions imposed on Jewish immigration into Palestine, but on the other hand it was driven by its financial difficulties to open up discussions with the Zionists — as had its political rival, the liberal Entente — as a way of bargaining over any liberalization of these measures. It had enough confidence in its political power to not share Abdul Hamid's fears about the possible consequences of Zionism. Arab politicians remained in large part anti-Zionist and denounced what they saw as full-blown collusion between the Zionists and the Unionists, often supporting their argument by pointing to the important participation in the Committee of the *donmes* from Salonica, who were descendants of a crypto-Jewish sect. Yet those who had the broadest view of things, and who also had the least contact with local reactions, had in mind a union of separatist nationalist movements against the Ottoman centralism of the Young Turks. In this perspective, the Zionist movement, which had at its disposal powerful financial means and numerous personalities who were both on a high intellectual level and had a great deal of political experience, could be of great help to the young, inexperienced, weak, and poor Arab nationalist movement. Discussions were carried on and continued with deceptive vicissitudes until 1914. Following one resounding setback, Nassif Bey al-Khalidi, the Arab engineer from Jerusalem who was an advocate of Arab-Zionist agreement, made a disillusioned and perceptive warning that has been found in the Zionist archives. In French, he told Dr. Thon of the Zionist Bureau in Jaffa:

"Be very careful, Messieurs Zionists, governments disappear, but peoples remain."[48]

The Zionists were hardly concerned at all about the reactions of the Arabs — and it is here that the unconsciously imperialist element in their thinking stands out. "The Jewish immigrants came to Palestine believing it to be a desolate, sparsely inhabited country. They were too busy with their own business and too ignorant of Arabic to notice what was going on around them. Since it was the Turks who ruled Palestine, they turned all their attention toward the Turks. This approach did not help make the Jews popular with the Arabs."[49]

The end of World War I, coming at a time when the Arab national movement was becoming a factor of prime importance, made a few Zionist Jews take cognizance of the significance of this problem. This factor, hardly even noticed before, strengthened the convictions of many non-Zionist Jews, who made some very perceptive warnings. [50] This was not enough to radically alter the attitude of the Zionist leaders, who were urged on by the very logic of the position they had started out with. They essentially viewed the Arab national movement as something dependent on Great Britain,[51] disregarding the real — and especially the potential — mass base of the Arab leaders at that time; and while the latter were, in fact, sometimes simply British agents, more often they were men who were playing their British card with the same ulterior motives as the Zionists themselves. Yet it must certainly be recognized that their freedom of action and maneuver was limited by the need to not look like traitors in the eyes of the masses. Thus the deep feeling of the masses, even if it remained unexpressed, weighed heavily in the situation. By disregarding this element, which only became stronger as time went on, the Zionist leaders were revealing a frame of mind that the colonialist world view dominant in Europe at the time both explained and excused. This did not make it any less the same frame of mind, nor did it lead any less irrevocably to future catastrophes.

Settling the war was difficult, as we know. It was a series of sordid deals ("the whole disgusting scramble," said Wilson) against a background of more or less brutal reactions (depending on what was possible) on the part of the populations whose fate was being decided. Only the Turks were able to mobilize enough forces on favorable terrain to be in a position to have any real weight in deciding the outcome. The British had made promise after promise — all contradictory. This was due to changes in thinking and circumstances in the course of the war, and also to diverging points of view in the various instances. Because of competition between the French, the English, and the Czarist Russians, the Sykes-Picot Agreement had foreseen an international administration for Palestine. But up to a point the Russian Revolution rendered the agreement out-of-date and in need of revision. The tendency of the British to make sure they received territorial guarantees had only increased during the war because of several factors: the desire to make sure they had a rampart from which the Suez Canal could be protected, plans for "insuring a territorial continuity between Egypt and India,"[52] and a determination to hold back and counterbalance the French protectorate over Syria proper and Lebanon to which they had been forced to agree. The Balfour Declaration remained the main argument upon which the British could base their claims during the post-war bargaining. And the task of the English was made easier by the clear position of the Zionist executive committee favoring plans for a British protectorate over a French protectorate.[53]

Thus Britons and Zionists backed each other on the question of Palestine. This is not to say that the English paid no attention to the Arab clients they were counting on despite the disillusionments caused by British repudiation of promises made to the Arabs. The Arab masses were indignant, and occasionally this spilled over into brutal actions. The Arab chiefs thought it wiser to maneuver and try to get as much as possible, without refusing (despite a few fruitless attempts to look in another direction) to play their British card. All the more so since there were great personal advantages for them in this approach.

The foremost efforts by the Zionists to reach an agreement with the Arabs occurred during this period. Naturally, these were summit agreements. They fitted into

British policy in that they aimed, on the one hand, to reconcile contradictory promises that had piled up during the war, and on the other hand to set up a series of buffer states under British influence that would protect Suez on the Asian side, keep an eye on a worrisome Kemalist Turkey allied with an even more worrisome Soviet Russia, and offset the possible influence of that troublesome ally — France. It was on the advice of Allenby, commander-in-chief of the British troops, that Weizmann established contact with Emir Faisal, the son of Sharif Hussein and commander of the Arab troops, as early as June 1918, when the Turks still occupied almost all of Palestine. Weizmann and Faisal found common ground, and the following year, when the Peace Conference opened in Paris, they concluded a noteworthy agreement. Faisal, head of the delegation to the Peace Conference from Hejaz, and the only spokesman for the Arabs at the conference, was in a difficult situation. He was chiefly exposed to the hostility of France, which insisted that the Sykes-Picot Agreement be put into effect, and which looked with suspicion on a future Arab state influenced by England since it could serve as a catalyst to a nationalist awakening in French North Africa. Clemenceau had just agreed in principle to give Mosul and Palestine to Lloyd George in return for compensation. Before this private agreement could be ratified by the conference, agreement on the fate of Palestine had to be obtained from all parties concerned. Faisal's English friends, and especially Lawrence, were the only support he had in this strange world of European diplomacy into which he had all of a sudden been catapulted, and they were pushing him to reach an agreement with the Zionists. Weizmann had struck him as being likeable, and had been careful to "present the entire affair in as inoffensive a way as possible,"[54] which had also been the unchanging policy followed by Herzl and his successors. Faisal, who for the time being had nothing, was certainly tempted, much more than Arab historians will admit, by the idea of giving Palestine to the Jews in return for a large, independent Arab state that this small Jewish Palestine would

furnish with the most valuable technical aid. He played
a somewhat hypocritical game, since he could not hope
to get this policy easily accepted by the Arab masses
who provided his base, especially by those in Palestine.[55]
In short, it was a matter of allowing several thousand
Jewish colonists who had a higher level of technical skill
to settle next to a vast Arab state that was already rich
in ethnic and religious minorities, and to bring with them
the numerous advantages promised by the Zionist Organization. The deliberately vague slogan of a "National
Jewish Home" did not raise the questions of sovereignty
in a provocative way for the time being.[56] Weizmann
indicated his displeasure at hearing Tardieu, the French
representative to the Council of Ten, officially state in
February 1919 that France would not be opposed to
a British mandate over Palestine, nor to the creation
of a Jewish state. "We ourselves had been very careful
not to use this term," he writes.[57]

Both parties to the Faisal-Weizmann agreement saw it
as a way of helping to get the Peace Conference to officially recognize their respective goals. Faisal wanted
a great, independent Arab kingdom, and Weizmann
wanted to get as far as possible along the road toward
Jewish colonization of Palestine and an autonomous Jewish territory under an English protectorate. The former
yielded to English protection as a way of attaining his
goal, especially in opposition to France, and the latter
sought this protection as a defense against possible enemies of his plan. Faisal accepted Jewish colonization in
Palestine in advance as being potentially advantageous.
He felt his acceptance could serve to win the agreement
first of Great Britain, and then the allies, for his own
plan. But he was not blind to the possible dangers of the
pact they had made; when warned about hostile reactions
by local Arabs, he was careful to add a postscript to the
agreement that was "perfectly understandable in light of
the extent to which he was involved," as Weizmann objectively recognized.[58] This postscript made everything
depend on the granting of Arab independence. The least
modification or the slightest deviation from the demands

made in his memorandum of January 4, 1919, would again place a question mark over the entire agreement. [59] But for the moment the agreement existed. "I think it is proper to say," admitted Weizmann, "that the existence of that agreement had much to do with the positive attitude of the Big Four toward Zionist aspirations."[60]

Without going into the complex details of the negotiations that followed, the thing to remember is that it all led to the mandate over Palestine that the League of Nations granted to Great Britain on July 24, 1922. This mandate explicitly ratified the Balfour Declaration in the name of the world community and gave the mandatory power "the responsibility of setting up a political, administrative, and economic state of affairs in the country such as to insure the establishment of the national home for the Jewish people."[61] It designated the Zionist Organization as having certain responsibilities in terms of Palestinian administration as far as Jewish questions were concerned.

From these facts, the following conclusions seem to me indisputable. Efforts to carry out the Zionist plan only got under way because of a political decision made by Great Britain under pressure from the Zionist Organization. In order to get support for its general policy from what it saw as an effective pressure group consisting of Jews in the Russian Empire and the United States, Great Britain went along without asking many questions about the real links these Jews had with political Zionism. It also went along because the decision in question appeared to serve its interests in a Near East that had just emerged from the war, and that is the way the Zionist leaders presented the matter. Great Britain felt that this course could be reconciled, at least in the long run, with its support for the Arab princes of the Hashemite dynasty and with their support for Britain in return.

The Zionist leaders helped bring about this reconciliation by playing down, for the time being, their plan for a Jewish state, and by being content to call for settlement facilities in Palestine and for the right of free immigration. In short, the Arabs were most justified in regarding the transplanting of a new and foreign element on Palestinian soil (an element whose vast majority were Europeans at that time) as something imposed on them by a European power thanks to the military victory of one group of European powers over another group with whom the Ottoman Empire had been allied.

These conclusions must be considered basic. Actually, the Zionists tend to trace the beginning of the Jewish state to either the first Jewish colonization in Palestine during the first wave of immigration (the *First Aliya*) from 1882 to 1903, which places the emphasis on the autonomous movement of the Jewish masses; or to the so-called War of Independence in 1948, which puts the stress on the refusal of the Arabs to accept the UN partition decision and on the bad faith, if not avowed hostility, of England against which the terrorist struggle of the preceding years had been unleashed. Naturally, the role of Jewish colonization prior to 1914 was important. But the existence of 85,000 Jews in Palestine in 1914 (which fell to around 56,000 in the course of the war) played only a very secondary role in the adoption of the Balfour Declaration. Later, the demand for independence for the *Yishuv* (the Jewish colony in Palestine) was only conceivable on the basis of the fact that there were 539,000 Jews in Palestine, or 31.5 percent of the total population (in 1943), whereas the proportion had been only 11 percent in 1922.[62] This massive immigration had only been made possible because of British protection, obtained in the manner already described. It would have been inconceivable on such a large scale, and with the alarming claims it was making, under an independent Arab state free from external pressures. The Zionist leaders in the mandate period were well aware of this when they called for strengthening the regiment of British police and opposed the creation of any representative body that might reduce, however slightly, the authority of the high commissioner.[63]

Subsequent events show that Faisal would not have been able to enforce the agreement he had more or less been forced to accept unless there were a drastic reduction in Zionist aspirations. In any event, his bargaining was based upon an inner imperialist logic that destroyed not merely his hopes but the very conditions in which he would have had some chance of getting his people to go along with his approach. He had to beat a retreat, and the facts show that it was Great Britain that laid the basis for making a reality out of Herzl's dream, that laid the basis for the Jewish state—even if later on it regretted having done so.

The Arabs too had managed to acquire a basis for their future independence only because of British support. The very events that had laid the basis for the Jewish state had freed them from the Turkish yoke. But they were bitterly disappointed. Instead of the great, united independent state they had been promised, Arab territory in Asia was divided, subjected to the protectorate of two great European powers under the hypocritical cloak of the mandate, and saddled with numerous restrictions limiting their freedom to decide their own affairs in favor of the "rights" of a third party. Within the Arab kingdoms or republics placed under mandate, political organizations were able to develop with greater or fewer restrictions depending on the period and the area. Their national character, and their call for independence in a more or less distant future, were acknowledged. This also provided a basis on which a struggle around the demand of total independence could be built.

There was a mortgage on both sides. But the conditions for lifting it were very different. The demands raised by the Arab nationalist organizations were backed up by indigenous masses who were practically unanimous in what they wanted (except, to a degree, in Lebanon). The Zionist organizations, in contrast, had against them the majority of the country in which they wanted to set up a sovereign state. In order to change this situation, they would have to increase the proportion of Jews in the country, a proportion that was only growing slowly (11.1 percent in 1922, 17.7 percent in 1931, 28 percent by the end of 1936); and to accomplish this, they would have to seek out the good offices of the mandatory power.

The other possible solution, military conquest, which was advocated by the Revisionist Party, seemed unfeasible.

The situation did not change until after 1939. During the preceding twenty years, Great Britain had shown itself increasingly sensitive to Arab hostility toward the Zionist scheme. While it had once seen a solution lying in partition, and thus in the creation of a Jewish state in a part of Palestine, it now finally decided, in a *White Paper* dated May 17, 1939, to clearly state its hostility to any such solution, and especially to a Jewish state encompassing all of mandatory Palestine. It had in mind the creation of an independent Palestinian state within ten years in which the Jews would not constitute more than one-third of the population, and hence it placed limitations on immigration and the sale of land. On the other hand, events in Europe were making the limitations on immigration intolerable, and the Jewish base in Palestine was now strong enough to make possible the kind of independent action on the part of the *Yishuv* that the Revisionists had been recommending for such a long time. By the end of 1943, the Jewish Agency estimated the number of Jews in Palestine at 539,000 out of a total population of 1,676,571 — 31.5 percent. The Jewish state could now only be set up in opposition to Great Britain, and the forces of the *Yishuv* appeared adequate to the task.

In general, Zionist policy presented two faces, both growing out of a situation in which the Zionists found themselves established as a minority of colonists surrounded by a hostile population and under the authority of an outside power. Vis-a-vis England (which at the very least had to pay attention to the feelings of the Arabs, on whom part of its foreign policy was built), and also vis-a-vis world opinion, this minority had to continue the firm Herzlian and post-Herzlian policy and "present the entire affair in as inoffensive a way as possible." Later, it was possible to write: "The goal (of Zionism) has remained unchanged since Herzl — the transformation of Palestine into a Jewish homeland, the creation of a Jewish state. For tactical political reasons, this goal has not always been clearly stated. But the evolution of Palestine and of the Jewish problem in general has reached such a point that clarity has become necessary."[64] This was in 1946, on the eve of the war that was the logical outgrowth of the situation that preceded it. But twelve years earlier, one of the most eminent and informed Zionist leaders, Arthur Ruppin, who supported a policy of reaching an understanding with the Arabs, though he was in a minority on this question in the Zionist Executive, wrote:

At the time of the Balfour Declaration, some Zionists and some non-Jewish promoters of Zionism saw Palestine becoming a Jewish state, although this conception could not be found in the Zionist program, and this goal is still officially put forward today by the Revisionist wing of the Zionist Organization. The term Jewish state is ambiguous, but it can be interpreted as meaning that Jews want to rule the country. The fears of the Arabs about this, however, ought to have been allayed by the *White Paper* published by the British government in 1922, shortly before it was invested with its Mandate, in which it defines its Palestine policy as well as its concept of a National Jewish Home. This *White Paper* was accepted by the Zionist Organization . . . This statement by the British government ought to give satisfaction to the Arabs, even if the Jews refused to accept it. But the Jews themselves tried to allay the fears of the Arabs. The Zionist Congresses of 1921, 1925, and 1929 expressed a desire to cooperate with the Arabs and recognized the principle that neither nationality in Palestine must dominate the other or be dominated by it; it must be a state in which Jews and Arabs can live side by side as two nationalities with equal rights . . . .[65]

This history of the *White Paper* is indeed informative, but especially as an illustration in a Jewish context of what is called *katman* or *taqiyya* in Arabic, meaning the systematic subterfuge the unorthodox mystics practiced regarding their ideas and goals.

This first *White Paper*, or Churchill Memorandum, published on June 3, 1922, was in fact an official program that explained how His Majesty's government intended to apply the mandate it was going to be given. Violent reactions by the Arabs, in Palestine and elsewhere, had made clear that it would be necessary to seriously take this opposition into account and to interpret the Balfour Declaration accordingly. In particular, it was noted that: "Phrases have been used such as that Palestine is to become 'as Jewish as England is English.' His Majesty's Government regard any such expectation as impracticable and have no such aim in view . . . the terms of the (Balfour) Declaration [. . .] do not contemplate that Palestine as a whole should be converted into a Jewish National Home, but that such a Home should be founded in *Palestine*." (Original emphasis) The British government had never intended "the disappearance or the subordination of the Arabic population, language, or culture in Palestine." Finally, "when it is asked what is meant by the development of the Jewish National Home in Palestine, it may be answered that it is not the imposition of a Jewish nationality upon the inhabitants of Palestine as a whole, but the further development of the existing Jewish community, with the assistance of Jews in other parts of the world, in order that it may become a center in which the Jewish people as a whole may take, on grounds of religion and race, an interest and a pride."

Transjordan was separated from Palestine, and therefore from the zone where Zionist settlement could be carried out. Immigration would be limited in terms of "the economic capacity of the country at the time to absorb new arrivals." On the other hand, the intangible nature of the Balfour Declaration was asserted at the very outset, as well as the idea that the Jews would be in Palestine by virtue of a right and not of some special favor. [66]

The British government urged the Zionist Organization to give its official approval to this document before the British mandate over Palestine was formalized. It even made it conditional upon such approval. The Organization wanted, more than anything else, to have the League of Nations adopt the text of this mandate, which officially, in terms of international law, recognized the validity of the Balfour Declaration and sanctioned the English protection that was so necessary. It decided — unanimously — to practice "*katman*" out of the conviction that "if carried out honestly and conscientiously, [the *White Paper*] would still afford us a framework for building up a Jewish majority in Palestine and for the eventual emergence of a Jewish state." This was the thinking of even the most extremist of Zionists, the future founder of the Revisionist Party, whose reaction was welcomed with joy by Weizmann, who had feared he would remain intransigent. [67]

Thus this Zionist agreement to interpret the Balfour Declaration as ruling out the creation of a Jewish state was presented, along with the draft text granting Great Britain a mandate over Palestine, to the League of Nations and was ratified by it on July 24, 1922. But the Zionist leadership only accepted it with the intention of getting around it, of using it to set up a situation that would some day make inevitable the emergence of this Jewish state that was always in their thoughts but never (officially) on their lips. Only a minority of Zionist political leaders sincerely and resolutely set as their goal the bi-national state, equally balanced between the two ethnic groups, that Arthur Ruppin described as the official, acknowledged aim of the Zionist Organization.

However, this subterfuge was denounced by extremist Zionists as disastrous and as objectively orienting the leaders toward accepting the idea that a transition to the ultimate goal could be made gradually, painlessly, peacefully, and without any problems. This was the argument put forward by the impatient Vladimir Jabotinsky (who had nonetheless signed his name to the letter accepting the Churchill Memorandum) and the Revisionist Party he founded. The Revisionists demanded a radical revision of the mandate, the creation of a Jewish state on both sides of the Jordan as soon as possible (even if this required authoritarian and military methods), and the formation of a Jewish Legion that would make the attainment of these goals possible and that would provide protection for massive immigration without having to worry about Arab interference.

"Assurances from other Zionist groups to the effect that

they are striving toward the same goal but for diplomatic reasons do not mention it," writes an Austrian Jewish professor, "are not held worthy of credence by the Revisionists."[68]   Actually, it was Jabotinsky's thirst for power and his desire above all to take Weizmann's place as head of the Zionist Organization—an ambition denounced by Weizmann[69] —that drove him in this way to sow unjustified doubts about the thinking of the existing leadership.

But while the Zionist leadership protested to the outside world that it wanted to avoid the ultimate creation of a Jewish national state, internally it behaved as if such a state were the natural fulfillment of its plan. This was nearly fatal since the Zionist project had as its program precisely the remedying of a situation in which Jews were a scattered and unorganized minority, or one organized only as a subordinate community in a non-Jewish state, risking the loss of its members through assimilation if the society was open, subject to collective oppression if it was closed. The project attracted mainly Jews to whom this program appealed, especially in the very beginning when conditions for those who settled in Palestine were very difficult. And then too from the very start the Jews in Palestine constituted a *Yishuv*, i.e., an organized body of people, a colony that was as cohesive as possible and that remained turned in on itself. As early as 1910, the *kaymakam* (let's call him the sub-prefect), an Arab patriot hanged five years later by Jamal Pasha, wrote:

> The Jews do not mix at all with the Ottomans; they purchase nothing from them. They have their own special bank . . . In each village and colony they have founded a central committee and a school . . . The Jews also have a blue flag with a Star of David in the center . . . They fly this flag instead of the Ottoman flag . . . When the Jews come to the administrative authorities, they state that they are entered in the Ottoman registers (that is, that they are Ottoman subjects), but this is a lie and a fraud . . .[70]

The mandate granted to Great Britain provided, moreover, in Article 4, that "an appropriate Jewish agency shall be recognized as a public body for the purpose of advising and cooperating with the Administration of Palestine in such economic, social, and other matters as may affect the establishment of the national Jewish home and the interests of the Jewish population in Palestine." This body was to be the Zionist Organization for "so long as its organization and constitution are in the opinion of the Mandatory appropriate."[71]

In the Palestine of the mandate period, Jews were forced by the nature of things to mix more or less with the Arabs and the English, especially in the administration. In accordance with Ottoman practice and theory, which continued in force, the various ethnic and religious groups enjoyed a certain degree of internal autonomy. This is what is called the system of *millets*, which even today has been partially retained in Israel and Lebanon, particularly in the area of personal status under the law. But with the entry of the English into Jerusalem in December 1917, the Jewish community acquired what was properly speaking a political organization with a Provisional Committee that gave way in October 1920 to a kind of Constituent Assembly with an Executive Committee. The organization was ratified by a British regulation (December 30, 1927), which was amended on March 1, 1930, after arduous negotiations with the representative assembly (*asefat hanivcharim*, "Assembly of Deputies"). This in turn each year elected a general council (*Va'ad Leumi*, National Committee) responsible to the Assembly, which chose an executive from its midst. Thus there was actually a kind of government for the *Yishuv* with almost the powers of a state over those who recognized its authority (which did not include, for instance, anti-Zionist religious extremists). The Assembly could levy taxes on those under its control. It organized the social activities of the *Yishuv* and was responsible for its public education and indirectly for its religious organization. On the eve of the Palestine War, the government of the *Yishuv* could thus organize

a system of military service among "those under its ju-
risdiction."

Thus the *Yishuv* formed a bloc, divided by often serious
internal quarrels, but united as a whole in the face of
the outside world, and possessing bodies that expressed
this quasi-unity. On the other side, the Arabs were divided
into several religious communities, Moslem and Christian,
linked together only by constantly changing and opposing
political parties. The Jews were also united by semi-auton-
omous networks in the economic sphere—cooperatives,
a central distribution organization, and unions brought
together in the powerful *Histadrut,* which also served
as capitalist entrepreneur, banker, insurance agency, and
landowner, and which operated a kind of social security.
And so in 1946 a Lebanese was able to defend a doc-
toral thesis at the French School of Law in Beirut on
"The Formative Elements of a Jewish State in Palestine"
by taking up the *Yishuv's* state-like characteristics.[72]

Therefore, as indicated above, the struggle for the ultimate goals could be begun once the organizational foundation of the Jewish state was well in place, and once
the immigration carried out as a result of and under the
protection of the British mandate had increased its demo-
graphic base to the point where it comprised one-third
of the total population of the country. This struggle took
place in two stages. Although very few Zionists had come
from Great Britain, this country, in regard to Palestine,
played the role of mother country for a colony that was
being settled, because, like it or not, it had protected the
formation and growth of the *Yishuv* as it had, for example, once protected British colonization in North
America, and as France had protected French colonization
in Algeria. The classical pattern in such situations is
that tensions often arise between mother country and
colony over regulations imposed by the mother country
that the colonists frequently find annoying, and over legislation that they do not control, at least not entirely,
and that often strikes them as being "out of touch" with
local conditions. This is especially true when the mother
country thinks in terms of foreign policy on a world scale

but has to take into account the interests and aspirations of the native population. The fact that the Jewish Palestinian colonists had not come from the British population at all, and the fact that their means for applying pressure on the British government, while real, were far fewer than those the *Pieds Noirs* were able to use on the French government, for example, only made London more inclined to sacrifice them. The historical conjuncture had made Arab interests much more valuable to the English than those of the *Yishuv*. The shape of events on the eve of World War II pushed the British to turn their backs on the half-measures of the past few years, and to publish a White Paper that did not completely satisfy the Arabs, but that took a position squarely opposed to the hopes of the Zionists.

The first revolt was therefore directed against Great Britain. The limitation of immigration under the atrocious conditions of the great massacre of Jews in Europe lent the call to battle a humane quality without equal both within and even outside the *Yishuv*. As is well known, this battle was fought with terrorist methods, the only methods available to the Jewish colonists at that time. It greatly strengthened their cohesiveness and their more or less clandestine military organization. It was definitely a war for independence, but by the *Yishuv* against Great Britain. The native inhabitants (who amounted to two-thirds of the entire population) remained onlookers, their own hopes for independence preventing them from taking the side of either of the "belligerents."

The radicalization of the anti-British struggle began with extremist Jewish groups (the *Irgun* or *Etzel*, and especially the *Lehi* or Stern group) who truly looked on the British as oppressors and harbored toward them the classic reactions of colonial subjects toward colonizers who forcibly maintain a people under their yoke. [73] The founder of the *Lehi*, Abraham Stern, pushed this logic to the point of advocating an alliance with all of Great Britain's enemies, including the USSR and, it seems, even Hitler. [74] This state of mind could only have arisen in a very different situation from the one that prevailed twenty years earlier when the English were on the whole the protectors of a scattered population surrounded by a hostile world. They were protectors who could be reticent and even spiteful, and whose protection did not negate the need to organize one's own independent local defense force, but protectors nonetheless without whom one could not get along. It is not surprising that these movements made inroads especially among young people. Little by little their approach won over the Jewish masses of the *Yishuv* as a whole, who were mobilized in the semi-official army, the Haganah, an outgrowth of the self-defense groups, which were usually limited to carrying out defensive activities. The struggle for freedom of immigration for the unfortunate refugees from the Nazi-controlled areas of Europe won over everyone, and the British restrictions, as well as the repression of terrorist activity with its usual internal logic, made the English "imperialist yoke" loathsome to everybody. In the first stages of this period, the Zionist leaders had decided that it was time to openly state their goals. On May 11, 1942, a meeting of the American Zionist Organization at the Hotel Biltmore in New York adopted a program presented by David Ben Gurion, president of the Executive Committee of the Jewish Agency. This "Biltmore program" called for the establishment of a Jewish state throughout all of Palestine, the creation of a Jewish army, the rejection of the 1939 White Paper, and unlimited immigration under the control of the Jewish Agency alone. On November 10, 1942, it was ratified by a special committee of the Zionist Organization in Jerusalem and thus became the official program of Zionism. From now on, the official Zionist leaders differed from the extremists only over which tactic to use as a way of getting Great Britain to accept the common goal upon which everyone agreed: brutal pressure through terrorist activity or a mixture of diplomacy, based on services rendered, and blackmail.

From now on, the program calling for a balanced bi-national state, which a decade earlier had appealed to a rather large minority of the *Yishuv*, became outdated and only a few small groups of idealists and groups on the far left still supported it. The glorification of the struggle against "British tyranny" and the arousal of public conscience to new heights by the sacred task of saving the survivors of the Jewish tragedy in Europe had pushed the Arab problem into the background, where it was almost forgotten. In reading memoirs of the anti-British terrorist struggle, one is struck by the degree to which the young enthusiasts who wanted to deliver "their country" from tyranny were unaware of the "native population" — mere stage extras who melted into the background of the countryside — at least as potentially active subjects with their own claims to this same country. The increasing English support at this time for the Arab national demands being articulated above all by kings and big landowners (who were nonetheless voicing the deep aspirations of their entire people) caused these demands to be generally regarded as emanating from puppets whose strings were pulled in England. Even the idea of dividing the country — which the Arabs also rejected for opposite reasons — was indignantly rejected. It was implicitly assumed that in the future Palestinian state, which unlimited immigration would make Jewish, the Arabs would be faced with a choice between submitting to authority and leaving.

A war with the Arabs, which only an outside force could have prevented, was no more than the logical consequence of the program for a Jewish state. This had indeed been seen by those rare persons who retained their ability to think clearly while most Zionists were avoiding the problem. In 1946, the great Jewish philosopher Martin Buber reproached official Zionism for its policy of primarily seeking international agreements instead of trying to reach a local agreement, in Palestine, with the Arabs concerned; he wrote that the Biltmore program, "interpreted as recognizing the goal as being one of 'conquering' the country through international maneuvers, not only stirred up Arab wrath against official Zionism, but it also made all efforts leading in the direction of an understanding between Jews and Arabs appear suspicious to the Arabs, who believed that these efforts were covering up the real, officially admitted intention."[75]

Likewise, Judah L. Magnes, president of the Hebrew University of Jerusalem, wrote:

> A Jewish state can only be obtained, if it ever is, through war . . . You can talk to an Arab about anything, but you cannot talk to him about a Jewish state. And that is because, by definition, a Jewish state means that the Jews will govern other people, other people who live in this Jewish state . . . Jabotinsky knew that long ago. He was the prophet of the Jewish state. Jabotinsky was ostracized, condemned, excommunicated. But we see now that almost the entire Zionist movement has adopted his point of view . . . In his early writings he said: "Has a people ever been known to give up its territory of its own volition? Likewise, the Arabs in Palestine will not renounce their sovereignty without violence." . . . All these things have now been adopted by those who excommunicated him. [76]

The terrorist activity, and the pressure exerted by the Zionist Organization on the United States in particular, had convinced the British that the best thing would be to go away and leave the Jews and the Arabs face to face. The power revealed by the *Yishuv*, the strength of its local base and of its determination to win autonomy, and the effectiveness of its "war" against the English had convinced the world powers as a whole that peaceful coexistence between it and the Arabs was utopian. Even Stalin at one point had to assess the value of counting on it as an anti-British force, perhaps of having the USSR succeed Great Britain as protector. The UN adopted a plan for dividing Palestine between the two ethnic groups on November 29, 1947. It proved powerless to control application of the plan from the outside. The stated determination of the British to withdraw their troops — the only element capable of imposing peace — from Palestine on May 15, 1948, made the bloody confrontation inevitable.

In this three-tiered struggle, once the battle against the mother-country oppressor was ended, the battle against the oppressed-in-the-making could begin. To be sure, the colonial situation could have been left behind at this point and two states, recognized by the UN, could have entered into the realm of international politics. The Zionists reproach the Arabs for not having chosen this solution by accepting the UN decision, which even came with the progressive guarantee of the USSR.

I will not try here to determine what could or should have been done according to various moral criteria, but to explain the Arab reactions, which are so often not understood in Europe, and how they could be rooted in the very nature of the events. For the Arab masses, acceptance of the UN decisions would have meant unconditional capitulation to a European *diktat,* no different from the capitulation of the black or yellow kings of the nineteenth century before the cannons trained on their palaces. Europe had collectively sent the colonists, whose goal was to seize a portion of the national territory.

Throughout the period when an indigenous reaction could have easily kicked these colonists out, this reaction had been halted by the British police and armed forces mandated by the European-American nations as a whole. This reaction had been disarmed morally by the misleading assurance that it was only a question of peacefully settling a few unfortunate and harmless groups who would remain a minority. And then, when the real intention of these groups was being publicly unveiled, when the collective strength they had slowly built up under the protection of the mandate was becoming clear, the European-American world from the socialist USSR to the ultra-capitalist United States — united in spite of their internal differences — wanted to force the Arabs to passively accept the *fait accompli.* For the Arabs, the settling of the Second World War was a bitter repeat of the deceitfulness of the First. As at that time, promises made in return for their agreement or neutrality were betrayed once they had achieved their intended goal by a malicious coalition of Europeans, united by their complicity in having made pledges to a people who had demonstrated a certain amount of faith in them. Did not the 1922 mandate itself stipulate that there would be no infringement of "the rights and position of other sections of the popula- tion" (the non-Jews) (Art. 6)? And had not the American presidents Roosevelt and Truman promised, in letters to Ibn Saud on April 5, 1945, and October 28, 1946, that no decision concerning Palestine would be taken with- out *full consultation* between the Arabs and the Jews, and that nothing would be decided that was contrary to Arab interests?[77]   All these promises had now been violated. Thus, no Arab could openly disavow the response of the Arab Higher Committee of Palestine:

> Any attempt by the Jews or any other power or group of powers to set up a Jewish state on Arab territory is an act of oppression that will be resisted by force on the grounds of legitimate defense.[78]

Thus the Palestine War was not seen by anyone in the Arab lands as a war of liberation led by anti-British, and hence anti-colonialist, Jewish revolutionaries against pleasure-seeking feudal lords who pushed stupefied and mule-like peasants in front of them to safeguard their own class interests — as the version widely accepted by the European left would have it (a version I challenged thir- teen years ago, thereby winning insults in *Les Temps Modernes*). This is also the version A. R. Abdel-Kader attempts to paint within the framework of a general view that is, quite frankly, delirious. The war could not even be seen as a struggle between two formerly colonial states, as could, for example, the struggle between Pakistan and India over Kashmir. In the latter case, each of the two parties is more or less supported, with greater or fewer ulterior motives, by one or another group of powers whose support fluctuates in keeping with changes in the international and local situation. Each of these groups, or each of these powers, seeks to use the conflict to strengthen its own influence — an influence that obviously makes use of the technical and economic superiority of the industrial world. But no one seeks to entrust the sov- ereignty of a portion of the Indo-Pakistani subcontinent to a population foreign to this subcontinent and coming from the European-American world itself. Seen with Arab eyes — and I believe I have shown this is not without objective justification — the Palestine War was a struggle against a new imperialist encroachment on the territory of a colonial people.

That is, at least, how it appeared in the eyes of the Arab masses. No one can honestly deny the real indignation felt by the Arab people, especially in Arab Asia, which was most directly concerned. The fact that the Egyptian peasants who were mobilized displayed little interest or understanding of the struggle did not mean that they had any sympathy for the Jews. For every element of the population however slightly politicized, whether through circumstances or education, felt that they were face to face with an invader. It is true that the Arab armies enjoyed some British support on various levels. But this support, which was clandestine and non-official, was also limited. During the tragic period between the UN partition decision and the British withdrawal, it amounted principally to the presence of English soldiers who were left without clear instructions, or received contradictory ones, and who had become accustomed during the preceding long phase of Jewish terrorism to regard the Jews as enemies.[79] As the (Ben-Gurionist) Zionist historians Jon and David Kimche write: "The Jews could not understand that they were reaping the reward of the unremitting terrorist activities of the two dissident organizations: the *Irgun* and the Stern group."[80] Hence, many decisions on a local level favored the Arabs. In a series of cases, the English soldiers warned the Arabs of imminent English evacuation of a garrison, thereby (often) permitting the Arabs to seize it. Numerous British weapons seem to have found their way into the hands of the Arabs in such cases. However, the instructions received by local British troops from their command were simply to concentrate their forces to avoid any new losses, to take back as much military materiel as possible, to withdraw with a minimum of friction by leaving each district in the control of whichever community was best situated on a local level.[81]   The few really military engagements by the British before their departure stemmed from an attempt (which failed) to prevent a Jewish take-over of points inside the zone allotted by the UN to the Arabs, for example at Jaffa.[82]

Great Britain's policy was inspired by considerations that went far beyond aid to the Arabs, in particular by the cold war situation at the time and British relations with the United States, as well as by the serious economic crisis that was shaking Britain. During the same period, the English withdrew from Greece, Burma, and India.[83] As usual, the various British ministries held divergent points of view on the matter, but they went along with the political orientation of the cabinet—to get out of the Palestinian quagmire. It seems that it was only later, with the unforeseen evolution of events on a local level, that certain British circles got the idea that things would end up with Great Britain being asked to play the role of arbiter in conditions it would find much easier than those prevailing near the end of the mandate. The very day after the partition plan was announced, on November 30, 1947, at dawn, Arab attacks announced the Arab refusal to accept the Jewish state. The guerrilla struggle began right away, in the presence of the British soldiers, who observed a neutrality that was somewhat partial to the Arabs. It began on a relatively small scale at first, with individual murders by snipers, dynamiting of buildings, reciprocal bombings, attacks and reprisals, with the latter carried out especially in the beginning by the *Irgun* and the *Lehi*. As the Zionists Jon and David Kimche say, "in the sequence of events, it quickly became difficult to say which were the attacks and which the reprisals; but all grew out of the Arab decision to reject the UN vote."[84]   The Arab Liberation Army volunteers, who, several thousand strong and led by Fawzi al-Kaukji, had been in Palestine since January 1948, launched several fruitless attacks against the Jewish colonies. The attacks, gambits, skirmishes, and riots to which this army resorted were used to justify Jewish reprisals on a wider scale. At first these reprisals were carried out mainly by extremist right-wing dissident formations such as the *Irgun* and the *Lehi* or Stern group, which accused the Jewish Agency's semi-clandestine official army, the *Haganah*, of passivity and even of complicity with the British. The official Zionist leaders did, in fact, hesitate to abandon completely all recourse to international backing, from the United States and even at times from Great Britain, hoping that in one way or another the UN would insure a painless transition to a Jewish state—or, if absolutely necessary, a bi-national state with a large Jewish majority; they were also prepared again, if necessary, to settle for the territory alloted by the UN partition plan, at least for a while. In the beginning, they wanted above all to demonstrate that they were capable of defending the Jewish zones and consequently that a Jewish state was viable.[85] The intensity of nationalist extremism among the Jewish masses—orchestrated by the *Irgun* and the *Lehi*, and raised to a new pitch first by the damage done by the Arab irregulars and then by their more systematic attacks in an effort to blockade Jewish Jerusalem in particular—swept the official Zionist leaders too into the onslaught, first through less and less selective reprisals designed to serve as spectacular "warnings" to discourage possible Arab attacks, and finally to make sure the Jews possessed as much land as possible by the time the British left. The main attacks were directed against Jaffa—which the UN plan left as an Arab enclave inside Jewish territory, but which was also like a pistol pointed at Tel Aviv—as well as toward liberating the Jewish sections of Jerusalem (international territory according to the same plan) and the road linking it with the Jewish regions.

Throughout this entire period the Arab states held conference after conference. They were very little inclined at the outset to get deeply involved in the affair for the most part, hoping that a mere show of force would cause the Jews to capitulate and that an agreement would follow that would leave them less territory than the UN had given them. This was also one of the rare coherent ideas to emerge among certain governmental authorities in London. The decisions by the Arab states to intervene were brought on by a collision of interests among themselves, by the ambition of Transjordan's King Abdallah to extend his domains to the areas on the west bank of the Jordan River, and by the desire of the others to stop him or at least reduce the extent of his acquisitions. Abdallah tried twice, in secret meetings with Golda Myerson [later changed to Meir — Editor], to persuade the Jews to reach an understanding with him, and his suggestions, though officially rebuffed, were not without effect. Contacts between the Political Department of the Jewish Agency and eminent Arab politicians who were among the least bellicose contributed to convincing the leaders of the *Yishuv* that they had no reason to fear outside intervention. They underestimated the effect of fear at seeing a Greater Jordan created under British protection; and above all they underestimated, once again, the main factor making intervention inevitable — the pressure of a burning Arab nationalism upon the rulers and the politicians. [86]

The regular Arab armies that entered Palestine beginning on May 15, 1948, had long-range attack plans, but, with rare exceptions, they were only able, in the last analysis, to occupy a portion of the zones left to the Arabs by the UN plan. [87] Most came from countries that had long been occupied by the British and had been furnished with British arms from the time they were formed. The Transjordanian army, known as the Arab Legion (with 6,000 men, of whom 4,500 were available for use in Palestine, according to Glubb, 9,200 according to I. Beer), had been commanded since 1939 by the English major Glubb Pasha serving in a Transjordanian capacity. All the Arab armies involved had at their command a total of about 25,000 soldiers, facing, at the outset, roughly the same number of Israeli soldiers, whose lines of communication were much shorter. [88] But in July there were 60,000 Jewish soldiers against 40,000 Arab soldiers. [89]

The Arabs were defeated as a result of a series of factors, not the least of which were the divisions between the states participating in the "coalition," the lack of military experience, and over-confidence.[90] In the beginning, their official armies had quite a rich supply of weapons, certainly much richer than the Haganah's. But the embargo decreed by the UN (after May 29) was observed by Great Britain, which alone was in a position to supply munitions and spare parts for the British-made weapons that most of the Arab armies were using.[91]

The Arabs had no weapons or munitions factories, while the Jews were producing certain weapons like mortars and mortar bombs. Above all, despite the embargo the Jews possessed substantial supplies of Czechoslovak and other weapons. The Haganah's networks in America and Europe benefited from widespread collusion and were able to organize the purchase and delivery of weapons and the recruitment and transportation of volunteers and mercenaries with incomparable ingenuity, great gusto, and the secret help of official authorities, as in France and Yugoslavia for example, despite the opposition of the United States and Great Britain. A ship carrying Czech arms to the Syrian army was sunk by a Haganah commando in the Adriatic near the Italian coast it had just left. While the Egyptians were able to buy arms from Italy and no doubt benefited from British collusion, the two truces imposed by the UN seem to have especially aided the arming of the Jews.[92]

On the whole, and without trying to unravel all the details of the obscure accusations hurled back and forth, it is clear that the unfolding of the war did nothing to dispel the Arabs' feeling that they were confronted by a powerful colony backed by the European-American nations as a whole. These nations, indeed, constituted the true mother country of the *Yishuv,* and, regardless of their ideological differences, they played their role by completely favoring the *Yishuv,* despite efforts by the British and American governments to be neutral, despite the UN administration, and despite the few active sympathizers of the Arab cause in Europe and America, who were among the most questionable and justifiably detested elements in their countries. The supporters of the Arab cause were of practically no use whatsoever to Arab military activity, while Israeli activity utilized to great advantage its innumerable sympathizers in the collective mother country.

The existing situation in the State of Israel has not refuted this analysis. The *Yishuv* has viewed — correctly — the Arab minority within its borders as a potential fifth column. The discriminatory measures taken against it flowed logically from this viewpoint. [93]

Let us conclude this quick sketch. The settling of a new population of European origin in a Palestine inhabited by Arabs was the product of a European ideological movement and was carried out under the influence of the pressure group that it represented. It achieved its ultimate goal — domination of the territory settled by the immigrants — thanks to a British political act, the Balfour Declaration, which was given the force of international law by the victory of the Allies over the Ottoman Empire and their decision to go along with the British commitment; thanks also to the protection provided by the British mandate, which made the development of an adequate base possible; and finally, thanks to a war directed first against a Great Britain become reticent, and then against the Palestinian Arabs supported by their fellow Arabs. This two-fold struggle was won thanks to the power of the *Yishuv's* sense of nationhood, its predictable superiority in European techniques of weaponry and organization, its ability to apply pressure in Europe and America, the guilt that Europeans and Americans felt at the crimes committed by the Germans — their European brothers — and their desire to exonerate themselves without great inconvenience and at the sole expense of other, non-European, parties. Throughout this entire process, the aspirations and interests of the native Arab population were taken into account by the Zionist leaders in only the most secondary fashion. The international point of view gained supremacy over the intranational point of view (inside Palestine), as Martin Buber put it. Even the fleeting agreement between Faisal and Weizmann occurred in relation to the broad policies of the great powers. Obsessed by his desire to obtain a great Hash-emite kingdom at any price, Faisal was ready to make a deal giving virtually all of Palestine to the Zionists in return for Jewish diplomatic, financial, and technical support for the future great Arab state he would head, thus sacrificing the part to the whole, in line with tra-ditional dynastic policy. His "moderation" could not suc-ceed because, unlike past rulers, he needed the support of the Arab masses in the Near East for his demands. But nothing could win the Syrian nationalists, and still less the Arabs inside Palestine, to his views on surren-dering Palestine. The commander was obliged to follow his troops. The relative "good will" of his brother Ab-dallah a quarter century later, which was the product of similar considerations, saw its results canceled out largely by the same factors.

The advancement and then success of the Zionist move-ment thus definitely occurred within the framework of European expansion into the countries belonging to what later came to be called the Third World. Given the ini-tial aims of the movement, it could not have been other-wise. Once the premises were laid down, the inexorable logic of history determined the consequences. Wanting to create a purely Jewish, or predominantly Jewish, state in an Arab Palestine in the twentieth century could not help but lead to a colonial-type situation and to the development (completely normal, sociologically speaking) of a racist state of mind, [94] and in the final analysis to a military confrontation between the two ethnic groups. One can understand why the Zionist leaders repeatedly spurned peaceful compromises with the Arabs, fearing that these compromises would not guarantee that they would be the rulers of the future Palestine. [95] One also understands very well the response of Golda Myerson (Golda Meir), long Israel's minister of foreign affairs, who, at the pinnacle of honor, has remained faithful to the determined and narrow outlook of the militant Ameri-can Zionist she became at the age of seventeen. An American member of the last Anglo-American commission to carry out investigations in Palestine in 1946 asked her:

"If the Jews as a minority had the same privileges as those you are promising the Arabs as a minority, would you be satisfied?"

"No, sir," replied Golda Myerson. "For there must be one place in the world where Jews are not a minority." [96]

One cannot deny that there is an internal consistency to this kind of thinking, which focuses on one particular solution and looks with disdain on the rights of the other party. But neither can one conclude that it was the moral duty of the other party to give in, nor be surprised that this solution provoked violent reactions.

Depending on one's scale of values, one can find the goal commendable. One can deem the harm inflicted upon the Arabs imaginary, minimal, or compensated for by important advantages. One can find the means excusable or even commendable also. But one cannot honestly deny the framework into which this plan was set.

In the same way, it is possible to pass judgment on European expansion in different ways. The historian might not pass judgment at all, and might limit himself to merely taking note of it. But if one passes judgment, if one condemns, if one becomes indignant, and if one praises the reactions of the colonized peoples, then even the slightest consistency in reasoning would have to rule out two different standards of judging and evaluating. Even if I am included in the ranks of the schizophrenic by Mme. Elaine Amado Levy-Valensi, I persist in thinking that being Jewish does not automatically oblige one to use two different sets of weights and measures. Otherwise one must be frank and state that whatever the circumstances, a given group of people, namely the group to which one belongs, is always right — in this case, using both anti-Semitic and Zionist criteria — the Jews. This kind of belief in the infallibility of one's own "ethnic" group is a frequent phenomenon in the history of human groups. It is called racism.

Objections and Limitations

Having put the subject into this general perspective, it remains for us to examine the objections it stirs up. All, naturally, are based on real facts, and some of them lead to conclusions that limit or at least qualify our general definition of the process.

It is only in order to refresh memories that I will mention the historical rights to the land of Palestine that are said to have been bequeathed to all Jews, since I would not insult my readers by believing they could be impressed by this argument.

The last truly independent Jewish State in Palestine ended in 63 B.C. when Pompey became master of Jerusalem; the last gasps of the Jewish nation in Palestine date from the revolt of Bar Kochba in 135 A.D. The Jewish population of Roman Palestine thinned out as a result of the deportations and enslavement that followed the two big revolts, but especially through emigration (which was considerable even centuries before independence was destroyed) and through conversion to paganism, then Christianity, then Islam. It is very probable—and physical anthropology tends to show that it is true—that the so-called Arab inhabitants of Palestine (a majority of whom, moreover, are people who have "become Arab") have much more of the ancient Hebrews' "blood" than most of the Jews of the Diaspora, whose religious exclusiveness in no way prevented them from absorbing converts of various origins.

For centuries Jewish proselytism was important even in Western Europe, and was continued elsewhere over long periods of time. Historically, sufficient evidence of this can be found in the Jewish state of Southern Arabia in the sixth century, based on southern Arabs who had become Jews; the Turkish Jewish state of the Khazars in Southeastern Russia in the eighth to the tenth centuries, whose base was Turkish or Finno-Ugric and no doubt partly Slavic; the Jews of China who have become thoroughly Chinese; the Black Jews of Cochin; the Falashas of Ethiopia, etc. And, from an anthropological point of view, a glance at any meeting of Jews from different backgrounds will suffice to give an idea of the importance of foreign contributions. Even if the heterogeneous body of Jews throughout the world who until recently have preserved ties to religious Judaism were considered a permanent collective personality, despite the profound internal changes it has undergone, and if by virtue of this it were considered the heir to the old Hebraic nation, it would still be impossible from any reasonable point of view to grant it the rights to a territory whose population — applying the same criteria of a stable personality defined by an existing community — has totally changed, even though its component parts have remained largely the same. As Faisal and many others before and after him have observed, from this point of view the Arabs could just as well lay claims to Spain. The argument often put forward by the Zionists, of insisting on the undying hope of Judaism to return to Zion, is no more persuasive. It turns the private preoccupations of one individual into a law for another. However impressive these historical arguments may have appeared to certain persons of a religious bent or under the influence of nationalist ideology,[97] they contain nothing that can transform the introduction of a *foreign* element, to the detriment of an *indigenous* population (in the usual meaning of these terms), into a simple matter of a return to one's native country.

On the other hand, the socialist outlook that inspired a large part of the *Yishuv* — at least in its earliest waves, which were the ones that had the greatest influence on its collective ideology — cannot be denied. However, this socialist outlook can neither logically nor sociologically be used as an argument to deny the colonial character of the *Yishuv*. Those who do use it this way are, whether they are aware of it or not, following the traditional line of thinking in European socialism that the only kind of relations a socialist society can possibly have with other societies are those motivated by the most deeply-rooted altruism. This is ideological juggling of the worst kind. It has more or less been justified by referring to the metaphysical doctrine of alienation as developed by the young Marx, attributing serious deviations in the human personality to property relations alone, and no less gratuitously assuming that collectivizing the means of production was all that it would take to insure a return to a basically altruistic personality. This approach, quite hazy at first, acquired more or less theoretical shape from Stalinism. The most lucid thinkers in the socialist movement sometimes recognized its worthlessness and — rarely, it is true — expressed skepticism with regard to it: Engels and Lenin, for instance.[98] Recent events — and others less recent that it took de-Stalinization to refresh memories about or open the eyes of those affected by Stalinism to — ought to have dispelled any doubts about this. A society that internally ranks among the most democratic or the most socialist can quite easily have relations with the outside world that deny the rights of other societies. If one thinks about it a while, one can see that this is even a phenomenon that has occurred very frequently throughout history, and that, sociologically speaking, it is quite normal, however depressing this may be for those who expect much from humanity.

The theoreticians of Jewish nationalist socialism paid very little attention to the societies their project threatened to hurt or destroy. Following the line of thinking we have just described, they naively thought that a renewal of the Jewish community could have only a beneficial effect on these societies and that as a result it was pointless to deal concretely with the question of what relations should be established with them. The analogy with the mental attitude of the French colonizers, imbued with the democratic ideology of the French Revolution, is obvious. It was for their own good that the Algerians and the Tonkinese were subjugated. In this way they would be prepared little by little for the day when later — much later — they would understand the Declaration of the Rights of Man and when, still later, it could be applied to them too.

It is certainly true that through the humanitarian values it brought to the fore, socialist ideology disposed a certain number of those whom it most influenced to be concerned about the fate of the people they were in contact with. Thus, the most deeply committed socialist elements of the *Yishuv* were concerned about the Arabs. But the conflict in the recesses of their psyche between their humanitarian ideal and their plan for a Jewish rebirth on Palestinian soil led in most cases to illusory conclusions, thanks to a mechanism explained by psychoanalysis. Consolation was easily found in the inviting thesis that the Arab masses, subjected to "feudalism" and exploited by their fellow countrymen, stood only to benefit from the Jewish conquest, at least in the long run. They would be made, or prepared to be made, happy in spite of themselves. The fact that these were the same traditional colonialist arguments that were so rationally denounced when others used them went unnoticed. It is well and good that socialist consciousness during the mandate period succeeded in bringing an occasionally sizable minority of the *Yishuv* to a position of sincerely supporting a balanced bi-national state. But, naturally, the settlement of the *Yishuv* in Palestine could not be called into question by the very people who were doing it. Only the influence of Stalinist ideology was such that it prompted a few rare individuals to take extreme positions and actions along this line. The circumstances in which the armed struggle took place between 1940 and 1948 mobilized nearly everyone behind efforts to protect and insure the autonomy of the *Yishuv*, sweeping aside all scruples in the process. As usually happens in this kind of conflict, the nationalist extremists ended up winning over almost the entire community.

In the conditions that have prevailed since 1948, the thesis that there is socialism in Israel has served to give the great majority of Israelis and their friends on the left the same kind of good conscience that, for example, the internal political democracy existing inside France gave to the French colonists in the colonies. Every conflict they become involved in readily becomes a conflict between good and evil.[99] It is thus amusing to see the most obviously "bourgeois" Zionists answer any criticism of Israel by waving the banner of Marxism and socialism. Thus the official organ of French Zionism, *La Terre retrouvee* [The Recovered Land] which generally is not at all oriented to the left, shows no restraint in praising A. R. Abdel-Kader as a "true Arab communist" for opposing evil souls who might claim to be communist or socialist while criticizing the Hebrew state.

I do not intend to analyze the respective proportions of the state, cooperative, and private sectors of the Israeli economy. I quite willingly admit that the Israeli collectivist colonies have often provided an example — perhaps the most advanced example ever seen — of the virtues that can be developed by a communitarian life style inspired by humanist ideology — even if it forms an integral part of a nationalist whole. I am leaving aside the problems of the relative weight of this economic sector and this ideology, and their influence in Israel. These problems are in fact not at all pertinent to this study. That kind of ideology may produce an inclination among members of an elite who subscribe to it to better understand the problems of the other side. But unfortunately, historical experience shows that Satan's bag is full of tricks; I am referring to the human propensity for seeing to it that the aspirations and interests of one's own group gain the upper hand over those of another, and to subsequently justify this outcome with the most idealistic arguments. This is one of the great lessons taught by Marx, although he himself at times ignored it. In 1916, Lenin, who was more realistic, spoke of this tendency to "ride on the backs of others," which was to be expected even after the social revolution.[100] It is true that up to a certain point this leads to an acceptance of the notion of human nature[101] that Bakunin counterposed to Marx, a questionable notion for the most part, and the use of which has been very harmful. It can, however, be neither totally accepted nor rejected.

Thus, even if one were to grant that the State of Israel is perfectly socialist from all points of view, one could by no means conclude as a result that its foreign policy was above criticism or that the attitude of the majority of its inhabitants was motivated by the purest internationalism with regard to other peoples.

From both a sociological and a human point of view one can understand the indignation of Israeli socialists when they are blamed for the imperialist, colonialist, or capitalist positions of Herzl or of one or another of his predecessors or successors. It is, indeed, certainly true that the masses who provided the strength and vitality of the Zionist movement, and without whom the Zionist organizations would never have had a real base, were very deeply influenced by socialist ideals and were very opposed to these Herzlian concepts. But, on the one hand, only a numerically tiny and politically very weak elite was impelled by these socialist ideals to perceive, without either conscious or unconscious evasion, the reactions of the people whom the movement as a whole was hurting. On the other hand, and more importantly, this movement constituted a whole. The Zionist leaders achieved their aims in part through the pressures brought to bear by their more or less socialist mass base, but also through the foreign policy game they played. In the face of an Ottoman Empire that had remained relatively strong, or of an independent Great-Arab, Great-Syrian, or Palestinian state that had freedom of action, the pressure of the Zionist groups of eastern Europe would have been fruitless. At most, it would have led to the settlement of minority Jewish communities in Palestine that would have been forced to reach a modus vivendi acceptable to the Arab majority.

These conditions would have turned the majority of these Jews, who wanted more than anything to emigrate, away from their exclusive orientation toward Palestine. The pressure would have changed, while remaining just as powerful, and would have doubtless led other countries to seek ways of solving the problem of the Jews oppressed by anti-Semitic states by allowing massive immigration, perhaps even by providing some free territory for those who demanded an autonomous community where they could be among themselves, as the USSR attempted to do with Birobidjan in its early stages.[102] It should not be forgotten that today as in the past — as already in the Roman period and even earlier, in Persian times — the majority of the Jews freely *chose* the Diaspora. For a long time now there have been more Jews in New York alone than in the State of Israel, and the majority of the Algerian Jews who left their country chose France and not Israel. Be that as it may, whether they like it or not, Israeli socialists have been dependent on the policy of the Zionist Organization. To a large extent, it is their policy too.

We have seen how the revolt of the *Yishuv* against British imperialism must be viewed historically. It must be seen as a revolt by a community of colonists against a mother country whose goals differed from its own, a revolt facilitated by the fact that the colonists did not belong to the same people as the mother country. That this revolt played its part in helping to weaken the British empire is certain. But to draw all the conclusions from this that A. R. Abdel-Kader, R. Misrahi, Jon and David Kimche and others reach is to pursue an illusory method of argumentation. In no way can this revolt take credit for jolting the Arab independence movement into motion. This movement, which took shape during the first years of the twentieth century, had already at the end of the First World War backed the moves of the Arab rulers and of the Arab big bourgeoisie toward autonomy. It found expression in the great Egyptian revolt of 1918-1919, the tremendous movement of the Iraqi people in 1920, the anti-Zionist riots in Palestine as early as 1920 (repeated often thereafter), and the numerous Syrian-Lebanese movements against the French mandate, of which what is usually called the Druse revolt of 1925-1926 was only the most spectacular example. Under the pressure of this mass movement the dynastic rulers and the nationalist parties that led it were able to obtain a series of concessions from Great Britain and France which, though more or less deceptive, were designed to give the appearance of satisfying the demands it raised.[103] Among these concessions, moreover, was the 1939 British *White Paper* that was to pit the *Yishuv* against England. It was this movement that actually led to the independence of Lebanon and Syria in 1943 and 1945. All this, which was to continue and later lead to much more important results, dates from before 1948 and the independence of Israel.

To be sure, the struggle of the Jewish terrorists against England showed even their enemies the relative weakness of arrogant Albion and thereby gave them encouragement. But they had not waited for this sign before beginning their struggle, or even seeing it produce the first promising results. In all of this there is nothing that would lessen the colonial character of the Jewish settling of Palestine.

A whole series of arguments aim to show how far removed the example of the *Yishuv* and of Israel is from what are thought of as typical colonial situations, stereotypes of colonization that are currently popular.

"In place of a mother country, Jews chased from one country to another in Europe," object the Jewish students in France. We have seen what the facts are regarding this. The historical role of mother country for the *Yishuv* was played by Europe as a whole, which unloaded into Palestine elements it considered undesirable, just as it sent convicts to colonize Australia or Guyana. Great Britain was the motor force in that by force of arms it conquered the territory to be occupied, set up an administration there, and imposed what it is accustomed to call law and order. In return, it met with the anger of its "colonists" when it thought it could limit their progress toward completely controlling the said territory.

We are assured that the purchase of land from the local owners took place without plunder, that it was carried out in the most correct fashion, and that it often even resulted in the seller being paid overly favorable prices.

What was often involved was not the best land, but the worst. The purchase worked to the benefit of both the seller and the agricultural development of the country in general. There is an element of truth in these arguments. No one in fact denies that these lands were legally acquired, at least before the 1948 war. For obvious political reasons, neither the Ottoman government nor the British mandatory administration could permit any other course. But brutal confiscation of land is by no means a fundamental characteristic of colonization. In fact, throughout the entire world, lands that were colonized were acquired much less often through the use of direct force than through seemingly legal deals, with the privileged position of the colonizer allowing him to use ruses and legal detours to his own advantage.[104] Much more frequently, the mere fact of a European presence, with its economic and technical superiority, with its enforcement of laws that, however just in the abstract, were modeled on European conditions and not adapted to the colonial situation, was alone enough to guarantee the bare minimum of deals in land that would make it possible to develop a core of colonized lands under very favorable or preferential conditions. But everything was done properly through buying and selling. In British Africa, for example, confiscation of land was a quite exceptional phenomenon. Great Britain did not settle English colonists on Hindu peasant lands. Many other examples could be mentioned.

Yet in all these cases, no one hesitates to speak of colonialism. The legal correctness of the land purchases made by the Zionists can in no way, therefore, be considered an argument against the colonial character of the *Yishuv*. And since 1948 confiscations have taken place on a vast scale.[105] The surface area cultivated by the Jews has gone from 928 square kilometers in the mandatory Palestine of 1941-1942 to 3,240 square kilometers in 1961-1962 in the State of Israel[106] (which is smaller than mandatory Palestine—20,700 square km as opposed to 27,000). Israel's Arabs have lost 40-50 percent of their land since the war.[107]

It is also certainly true that the Arab fellahin are in general not directly exploited by Jewish landholders as were, for example, the Algerian fellahin in the service of the French colonists. There are few Arab agricultural laborers on Jewish lands.[108] There are more industrial workers in Jewish enterprises. What exists (in the countryside) is surely not an ethnic stratification in which the Arab population works in the direct employ of members of the Jewish population, to whom they hand over the surplus product of their labor.

But if direct exploitation of the native population occurs frequently in the colonial world, it is not necessarily always a characteristic of it. It was an exception to the rule for the English colonists settling the territory that was to become the United States to have native Indians working for them. The English in the East Indies were not landowners who exploited peasants, any more than they were, for example, in Australia or New Zealand. Moreover, in a certain number of cases, there either was for all practical purposes no native population or it was exterminated, as in Tasmania. Are there those who would, as a result, entertain the idea that British expansion into all these territories was not colonial in nature?

The relations between the Israelis and the Arabs have in fact been less relations of exploitation than of domination. Let us take an overall view of the matter, sticking to the bare minimum of what cannot be disputed. Whatever the particular motives in the flight of the Arabs from Israeli territory, which reduced their number from two-thirds to one-tenth of the population, [109] the general cause was undeniably the determination of the new settlers who infiltrated into Palestine little by little over a period of some sixty years, to become the ruling element in a Jewish national state. I quite agree that this was less a determination to rule over the Arab ethnic group than it was to rule over a territory. But since no one can claim that they were freely given said territory by the Arabs, it was clearly a question of a successful effort to impose their will upon the other side. I do not want to dwell here on the situation of the Arabs in Israel; for that, I refer the reader to the fine, sensible, and balanced, but also lucid book already mentioned, by Walter Schwarz. [110] In spite of the recent relaxation of the most blatantly discriminatory measures, it is obvious that the Jewish majority is imposing its rule on the Arab minority. "The main impression," writes a perceptive Jewish-American sociologist, "is that the sympathies of the Israeli Arabs lie in the highest degree with their Arab kindred and that Arab allegiance is not to the Jewish majority that now governs, but rather to their kindred in Egypt or Jordan who promise to free them. There may be many exceptions, but this is certainly the attitude among the majority of the Arabs." [111] This is a quite normal consequence of the situation, and it is difficult to see how it could have been otherwise. The Arabs in Israel, like the Palestinian Arabs who fled Israel, are in a situation that they have not accepted and that the *Yishuv* has imposed upon them by force. [112] Whatever justifications one might be able to find for this act, no one should be able to deny that it is a fact.

I will conclude by briefly mentioning the Arab argument that, in addition to its domineering role at home and, historically speaking, the colonial nature of the creation of its state, Israel participates in the economic exploitation of the Third World alongside the industrialized European-American powers and Japan as part of the world system that is referred to as imperialist. A study of the problem would require a great deal of space and attention to nuances. If one sticks to generalities, it seems obvious that Israel's technical superiority gives it possibilities for exerting economic pressure on underdeveloped economies. But on the other hand, these possibilities are greatly diminished by the smallness of its territory, its difficulties with its nearest neighbors, and perhaps especially its own economic dependence on the European-American powers. It is rather by political choice that Israel has generally turned up as an ally of the imperialist powers, and it can be said that this political choice was in large part imposed by the circumstances surrounding the formation and birth of the state. This was another almost inevitable consequence of the initial choice made by the Zionists. At least it made any other attitude difficult. Roughly speaking, it is certainly true that, as Herzl wanted, Israel constitutes a beachhead of the industrialized, capitalist world in an underdeveloped world.

As for the right of the Israelis to continue to exist as a national community on the land they acquired in this way, it lies outside the framework of the problem we have raised here. The only rights they can validly lay claim to are those based on their improvement of the occupied territory, the work they put into this effort, and the personal sacrifices they agreed to undergo in order to reach this goal. But that has nothing to do with defining as colonial the process whereby they settled there. The colonial origins of the Algerian *Pieds Noirs* did not prevent the FLN from recognizing their rights, and their departure was not the result of expulsion but of their inability to adapt to the new situation or of their refusal to accept this situation. Similarly, no one speaks of chasing the whites out of South Africa because of their colonial origins. They are asked simply to coexist with the Blacks as equals. To set oneself up as an autonomous ethnic group is more difficult. Sometimes the native ethnic group can be brought by force to the point of recognizing this autonomy, which then becomes legal with the passage of time. But one can only claim to have left the colonial process behind when the native group, as a result of negotiated concessions, comes to accept this autonomy.

I believe the preceding pages have shown that the creation of the State of Israel on Palestinian soil is the cul-
mination of a process that fits perfectly into the great
European-American movement of expansion in the nineteenth and twentieth centuries whose aim was to settle
new inhabitants among other peoples or to dominate them
economically and politically. This is, moreover, an obvious diagnosis, and if I have taken so many words
to state it, it is only because of the desperate efforts that
have been made to conceal it. What is involved here are
facts. As for terminology, it seems to me that the term
colonial process is very suitable, considering the obvious
parallel with phenomena everyone agrees to designate
in this way. But this is a linguistic question.

It is quite obvious that this is a colonial process with
its own special characteristics — as with many others,
moreover. There was settlement of colonists — unlike the
cases of India and Greenland, for example. The colonists
did not come from the mother country, which is also the
case, for example, with the island of Mauritius. A major
part of the native population was displaced, as was true
over a long period of time with the Indians in New England. Not all were left in a state of direct economic dependence on the colonists, but in a state of political dependence for those who remained inside Israel, while the
settling of the colonists and the setting up of the state
brought to the rest a fate over which they had no control.

The purpose of definitions is to justify labels by being
more or less comprehensive, depending on the facts and
subjects one wants to cover. It is no doubt possible to

find definitions of colonialism that do not cover the particular case of Israel. One of the definitions of the term "colony" in the *Grand Larousse encyclopedique* ("territory occupied and administered by a nation outside of its boundaries and remaining linked to the mother country by very close ties") is hardly suitable. Another ("a collection of persons who leave their country to go populate another") is, on the other hand, very adequate. The Hebrew term *Yishuv*, commonly used by persons with an interest in the subject, is defined by the Elmaleh Hebrew-French dictionary as: "inhabited country, colony, inhabited province; population; . . . colonization." It is true that this referred especially to colonies in the Greek sense. But a definition like the one in Quillet-Flammarion that has the contemporary period in mind (colony = "exotic country, generally subjugated by right of conquest and placed in a state of political and economic dependence on the conqueror") works very well. And, more profoundly, a sociologist, reviewing all known cases, concluded: "One can speak of colonization when there is, and by the very fact that there is, *occupation with domination;* when there is, and by the very fact that there is, emigration with legislation."[113] The Jews attracted by Zionism emigrated to Palestine, and then they dominated it. They occupied it in deed and then adopted legislation to justify this occupation by law. Everything is there.

What are the consequences to be drawn from this diagnosis? Preach holy war against the intruders and demand that they be forcibly evicted and cast into the sea in the name of a universal conscience that was very slow to condemn colonialism? Brand them as criminals in the eyes of the whole world? Demand that, barefoot and with a rope already around their neck, they come pleading for forgiveness for their original sin?

My argumentation, which has been limited to the area of facts, does not necessarily imply these kinds of conclusions. It leaves aside questions of passing judgment, of future political perspectives, and of possible courses of action. Nevertheless, I would like, only now, to express my own opinion. It is up to the Arabs, who are the ones who have been wronged, to determine what their policy toward Israel will be. The role of others does not seem to me to be to urge them to seek military solutions. The militant revolutionary approach has given rise to strange reactions. It is one thing to understand, and to make others understand, the feelings of rebellion that stir a people or a class in struggle, and to stand up to the hypocritical approach that condemns acts of rebellion by the oppressed in the name of some universal morality, while forgetting about the weight of the oppression and crimes of the oppressor. It is another thing to incite those who are more or less oppressed to choose a bloody solution before all else, and generally to do so from a safe and tranquil vantage point. At the risk of once again being branded with the pejorative mark of a humanist, I will say that I prefer bloodless solutions to the extent that they are possible, and that I do not recognize for myself the right to preach vengeance and murder from my ivory tower.

Colonists and colonizers are not monsters with human faces whose behavior defies rational explanation, as one might think from reading left-wing intellectuals. I am anti-colonialist and anti-racist, but I cannot on that account give up attempting to explain colonialism and racism in terms of the most widespread and common-place social and psychological factors, which no one should claim lie beyond reach. Belonging to a colonizing group is not the unspeakable and unpardonable crime it is thought to be in cafes along Saint-Germain and Saint-Michel boulevards. Who is innocent of this charge? The only variable lies in the time that has elapsed since the usurping was done. The human conscience sooner or later accepts the idea that long-time use establishes a valid claim. History is full of faits accomplis. Since Cromwell, British colonizers have occupied Catholic Ireland and colonized Ulster, which remained Protestant and where the Catholic minority is discriminated against. The Irish had sworn never to recognize this amputation of their homeland. No one doubts that the amputation was unjust, that it was obtained through force and consolidated through force. And then one fine day in February 1965, they recognized the existence of Ulster and the Irish president paid a solemn visit to Belfast. [114]

The Jews of Israel too are people like other people. Some of them have hammered out an illusory ideology to which they have sacrificed themselves as well as a great deal of effort and many human lives. They are not alone. Many are those who have suffered much but have looked with indifference upon the sufferings and rights of others. Many went there because it was the life preserver thrown to them. They most assuredly did not first engage in scholarly research to find out if they had a right to it according to Kantian morality or existentialist ethics.

It is accordingly useless to reproach them for it. The future depends largely on the relationship of forces, also in part on the awareness of how deep the problems are. It is that alone which justifies this study.

To be aware of the colonial character of the State of Israel is to begin to make clear why the pressure of the events does so much to thrust Israel into the camp of the Western powers, and why any other orientation would require heroic efforts on the part of progressive elements in Israel. Above all, it is to understand the reactions of the Arabs and peoples of the Third World who are in the same situation. Those who automatically classify all the Arab movements and regimes as fascist simply because they are opposed to Israel are spreading an erroneous and deeply harmful conception of the problem. Similarly, all those who hold to legends about a gratuitous hatred of Arabs for Jews, or the thesis of a consciously worked out Machiavellian myth, are misleading themselves and others. If there is indeed hatred that often exceeds all bounds, and if rulers and ideologists build myths around the question of Palestine as a way of mobilizing support, it is all based on an objective reality for which the Zionist leaders are responsible: the colonization of a foreign land. [115] A follower of nonviolence may be allowed to regard the revolt of the Arabs against a colonial situation as something to be condemned from a moral point of view, but the slightest intellectual consistency prohibits an anti-colonialist from making such a moral condemnation. At most, he can find this revolt premature for the time being.

It follows that it would be a dangerous illusion to count on a new social regime among the Arabs to accept Israel. Let it be said forthrightly, even if it hurts or arouses indignation among left-wing conformists who believe that the social revolution solves all problems. There is no "revolutionary solution" to the Israeli-Arab problem. The creation of the State of Israel was an outrage committed against the Arabs as a people. No regime can accept it of its own free will. International or internal political circumstances could perhaps one day force recognition of Israel. But this cannot be simply the product of an ideology that might concede that there were grounds for the Israeli colonization. On the contrary, it is those regimes that are most socialistically inclined that have also shown themselves to be the most adamant. To believe the opposite would be to reveal profound ignorance of local conditions or to be utterly misled by ideological passion. The riots in Jordan following the Israeli reprisal raid in the Hebron region (events that are unfolding as I am finishing this study) clearly show the dangers in the usual interpretation of Arab hostility toward Israel. How can those who explain it as an artificial creation of "fascist" governments and movements explain the depth of the Palestinian indignation revealed by these disturbances? How can they not notice that their interpretation ties in with the one that all colonialist states have used to justify their repression of indigenous liberation movements? And the Levi Eshkol government itself has obviously excluded the possibility that such a movement could develop. A victim of its own Zionist myths, it has been led by them to falsify the very realities of the problem it is confronted with. A classical, but dangerous phenomenon.

It is possible that war is the only way out of the situation created by Zionism. I leave it to others to find cause for rejoicing in this. But if there is any chance of some day seeing a peaceful solution, it will not be achieved by telling the Arabs that it is their duty to applaud their conquerors because they are Europeans or are in the process of becoming Europeanized, because they are "advanced," because they are revolutionary or (almost) socialist, and, even less, simply because they are Jews! The most that can be asked of the Arabs is that they resign themselves to a disagreeable situation, and that in resigning themselves they make the best of their resignation. It is not easy to get a conquered person to resign himself to defeat, and it is not made any easier by loudly proclaiming how right it was that he was soundly beaten. It is generally wiser to offer him compensation. And those who have not suffered from the fight can (and, I believe, even must) recommend forgiveness for the injuries inflicted. They are hardly entitled to demand it.

Notes to the Introduction

1. French edition published by Etudes et Documentation Internationales, Paris, 1968. American edition, with an introduction by Nathan Weinstock, published by Pathfinder Press, New York, 1970.

2. *New York Times*, July 14, 1969.

3. Cf. *Documents of the Palestinian Resistance Struggle*, Pathfinder Press, New York, 1971.

4. Quoted in "Palestine and the Jews" by Eli Lobel, essay in *The Arab World and Israel*, Monthly Review Press, New York, 1970.

5. Cf. "I.F. Stone Reconsiders Zionism," by Marie Syrkin, Golda Meir's biographer, in *Midstream*, October 1967.

Notes

1. *Falsafat ath-thawra,* Cairo, Dar al-Ma'arif, no date ("Ikhtarna laka" Collection, 3) p. 69; cf. French translation of Gamal Abdel Nasser's *La Philosophie de la revolution,* Cairo, p. 53f.

2. Ra'if Khouri, "Al-qadiyya al-falastiniyya" in *at-Tariq,* Beirut, March 31, 1946, p. 2.

3. *Mashrou al-mithaq,* 21 Mayou 1962, (Cairo), *maslahat al-isti'lamat,* p. 119.

4. *Al-Ahram,* April 2, 1965.

5. I tried to at least outline these nuances in my article "Les Arabes et Israel" in *Revue francaise de science politique,* vol. XVI, No. 4, August 1966, pp. 785-798.

6. *Le conflit judeo-arabe, Juifs et Arabes face a l'avenir,* Paris, Maspero, 1961 ("Cahiers Libres" Collection, 20-21). I made a lengthy and detailed critique of this in *Verite-Liberte,* No. 16-17, February-March 1962.

7. R. Misrahi, "Les Israeliens, les Arabes et la terre" in *Les Temps Modernes,* No. 147-148, May-June 1958, pp. 2183-2209.

8. *France-Observateur,* April 2, 1966, p. 8f.

9. In the article quoted above.

10. There is a great deal of confusion and many inaccurate generalizations in all this. Let us call attention, in passing, only to the fact that prior to World War I Palestine was con-

sidered geographically to be a part of Syria. Zionist leader Arthur Ruppin's remarkable report on the economic potential of the region takes as its title *Syrien als Wirtschaftsgebiet* [Syria as an Economic Region] (2nd edition, Berlin-Wein, B. Harz, 1920; the 1st edition was in 1917), although his objective is obviously to lay the groundwork for Palestinian colonization. The rural community with a periodic redistribution of lots is not the "Ottoman property system," but one of the forms of common tenure. Statistics are not available on how widespread it was. According to Ruppin (in the work already mentioned), the system was in the process of disintegrating and private property had been established in "many villages" of "Syria." The idea, repeated a thousand times over by Zionist propaganda, that Palestine was a desert at the beginning of the twentieth century, is absolutely false.

11. In his apologetic fervor, Misrahi blithely confuses the ban on absenteeism by the landlord with a ban on employing wage earners. I direct him to Zionist Andre Chouraqui, who writes: "The contracts [of the J. N. F.] are generally made with the following conditions: The farmer is obligated to work the land himself, . . . to recruit the agricultural or industrial labor force that will be needed to improve the land from among the pioneers of Israel." (*L'Etat d'Israel*, Paris, P. U. F., 1955, p. 98). In 1957, agricultural workers made up two-fifths of the work force in agriculture, and the rate was increasing due to the fact that they were a higher proportion of the new immigrants (S. Sitton, *Israel, immigration et croissance*, Paris, Cujas, 1963, p. 214). France, without any recourse to Biblical mythology, reached a position that was twice as revolutionary (using Misrahi's criterion) since only one-fifth of its agricultural work force consisted of wage earners.

12. Let's add to this the frequent stereotype, graphically captured by the caricaturist Dosh, which collectively portrays Israel as an underdog, an unfortunate, naive, and tiny people that does its best in the face of fierce and groundless hostility from all sides. It is an image that resembles (among others) the one of France, in the eyes of Michelet and Hugo, as the disinterested supporter of just causes that is crucified by preying powers as the sad result of a too generous idealism. All this amounts to nothing but nationalist ideological myths.

13. G. Delahache, "Un voyage d'etudes" (in *Cahiers de la*

quinzaine, 5th series, 6th cahier, Dec. 1904, pp. 69-116), p. 96.

14. S. M. Dubnow, *Die neueste Geschichte des judischen Volkes* (1789-1914), Berlin, Judischer Verlag, 1920-1923, 3 vol., vol. III; French translation Simon Doubnov, *Histoire moderne du peuple juif,* Paris, Payot, 1933, vol. II. The usual ideas about the history of anti-Semitism and the reactions of the Jews to it are often marked by the most deplorable ignorance, even among people who are intensely involved in the "Jewish problem" and who get their material on this subject published. Precise conditions that existed during the decades of Hitlerism tend to be transposed into the past. For information on the rebirth of anti-Semitism after 1881 and the exact political conditions that characterized it, see, for example, James Park's good popularization, *An Enemy of the People, Antisemitism,* Harmondsworth, Penguin Books, 1945 (*Penguin Books,* No. 521).

15. S. M. Dubnow, in the work already mentioned (German text), vol. III, p. 327 f.

16. Cf. the texts by Ahad Ha'am and Isaac Epstein (1907) quoted by M. Perlmann, "Chapters of Arab-Jewish Diplomacy, 1918-1922" (in *Jewish Social Studies,* New York, vol. VI, no. 2, April 1944, pp. 123-154), pp. 123-124.

17. Leon Pinsker, *Auto-Emancipation,* French translation by J. Schulsinger, Cairo-Alexandria, 1944 (Collection "Les ecrits juifs"), p. 69f.

18. *Ibid.,* p. 79f.

19. *Ibid.,* p. 92.

20. *Ibid.,* pp. 94-96.

21. *Ibid.,* p. 96.

22. Th. Herzl, *L'Etat Juif,* French translation, Paris, Lipschutz, 1926, pp. 92-95.

23. That is, the doctrine of Hovevei Zion, "the Lovers of Zion," a Palestinophile movement of Russian Jews beginning in the 1880s. Without involving any clear political outlook,

it sought to regenerate the Jewish people by establishing Jewish agricultural colonies in the Promised Land. The legal name taken in 1890 by the groups inspired by this ideal is significant: Society for the encouragement of Jewish agricultural and manual workers in Syria and Palestine.

24. "One of the people" (in Hebrew), the pseudonym of Asher Ginzberg (1856-1927), a Russian Jewish writer and one of the most impressive thinkers of the nationalist tendency. Political Zionism paid no attention to many of his warnings, and congratulates itself for not having done so. But the balance-sheet has not yet been drawn.

25. Herzl, *ibid.,* p. 23.

26. *Ibid.,* p. 95.

27. A discussion of this can be found, for example, in Marcel Bernfeld, *Le sionisme, etude de droit international public,* Paris, Jouve, 1920, p. 399 ff.

28. Text in Bernfeld, for example, *ibid.,* p. 427, n. 1. Plehve promises Zionism "moral and material support on the day certain of the practical measures it takes serve to reduce the Jewish population in Russia." An account of the congenial meeting between Herzl and Plehve is in Andre Chouraqui, *A Man Alone, The Life of Theodore Herzl,* Jerusalem, Keter Books, 1970, p. 230ff. Plehve was brought down the following year by the Social-Revolutionary terrorist Yegor Sazonov.

29. "My warmest adherent so far is the Pressburg anti-Semite Ivan von Simonyi . . ." wrote Herzl on March 4, 1896 (A. Chouraqui, *A Man Alone,* p. 106); Witte, the Czar's finance minister, explained to Herzl: "I used to say to Alexander III: 'If it were possible, Your Majesty, to drown the six or seven million Jews in the Black Sea, I should be perfectly satisfied. But that is not possible, so we must let them live.'" And, when Herzl told him that he was counting on certain signs of encouragement from the Russian government, he replied: "But we give the Jews encouragement to emigrate—a good kicking, for example . . ." (*ibid.,* p. 235f.) Herzl recognized: "They will hold it against me, with all the reason in the world, that I am serving the anti-Semites' purpose by declaring that we

are a people, one people." (*ibid.*, p. 199). In his vision of the birth of the State of Israel, he saw the "liberated" Jews acknowledging: "The anti-Semites were right. But let us not be jealous, for we, too, will be happy." (*ibid.*, p. 167; cf. also p. 215). I beg the reader to observe that all I am doing regarding Herzl's attitude is using his own *Jewish State* and his biography, written by the Zionist Andre Chouraqui. There is much more that could be said, for example, as the work of Mme. Leonhard (Arab-Dutch Institute), which is based on primary sources, shows. She gave a well-documented survey of it at the Mutualite on December 9, 1966.

30. Cf. the observations on this — still valid, in my opinion, in my "Stalinist" article, "Sionisme et socialisme" (in *La Nouvelle Critique,* No. 43, February 1955, pp. 18-48) p. 32f. Details ought to be added in particular dealing with the *Haavara* ("transfer") agreement between Hitler's Reich and the Jewish Agency to facilitate the emigration of German Jews to Palestine, cf. L. Hirszowicz, "Nazi Germany and the Palestine Partition Plan" (in *Middle Eastern Studies,* vol. I, No. 1, October 1964, pp. 40-65), p. 45f. and *Les Archives secretes de la Wilhelmstrasse,* V, book II, Paris, Plon, 1954, pp. 5, 25-28, 147, etc. "This German measure, dictated by internal policy considerations, virtually favors the consolidation of Judaism in Palestine and speeds up the formation of a Palestinian Jewish state," acknowledged a circular-telegram from the German Minister of Foreign Affairs dated June 22, 1937 (*ibid.*, p. 3). After discussion of this subject in various levels of the German administration, the staff adviser Clodius noted on January 27, 1938: "The question of emigration toward Palestine by the Jews of Germany . . . has once more, by decision of the Fuehrer, been settled in the direction of having it continue" (p. 28).

31. General outline in G. Lenczowski, *The Middle East in World Affairs,* 3rd ed., Ithaca, Cornell University Press, 1962, p. 67 ff.; more details in George Antonius, *The Arab Awakening, the Story of the Arab National Movement,* New York, 1965, p. 243 ff. and especially in the massive work by Leonard Stein, *The Balfour Declaration,* London, Vallentine and Mitchell, 1961.

32. Chaim Weizmann, *Trial and Error*, New York, Harper & Bros., 1949, p. 200.

33. *Ibid.*, p. 178.

34. This was not, as Weizmann believed, the only opposition to lead to a modification of the draft declaration in the direction of taking the rights of non-Jews a little more into consideration. But it did contribute to this.

35. Weizmann, *ibid.*, p. 205.

36. "Too long have you been tormented under the iron Muscovite yoke (*unter dem eisernen moskowitischen Joch*)," eloquently states the proclamation to the Jews of Poland from the High Command of the German and Austro-Hungarian armies in August-September 1914. The full flavor of this violent denunciation of the Czarist pogroms and anti-Semitism can be appreciated in light of subsequent developments (transcription of the Yiddish text in Latin script in H. L. Strack, *Judischdeutsche Texte,* Leipzig, Hinrichs, 1917, p. 9f.) The German and Austro-Hungarian Social Democratic parties are known to have also used the alibi of a struggle against reactionary and anti-Semitic Czarism as a way of justifying their support to their governments during the war.

37. Cf. Lloyd George's declaration to the Palestinian Royal Commission in 1936: "The Zionist leaders gave us a definite promise that, if the Allies committed themselves to giving facilities for the establishment of a national home for the Jews in Palestine, they would do their best to rally Jewish sentiment and support throughout the world to the Allied cause. They kept their word." Expanding on proof of this before the House of Commons in 1937, he stated that the Zionists "were helpful in America and in Russia, which at that moment was just walking out and leaving us alone" (quoted by Lenczowski in the work already cited, p. 81f.).

38. Details in L. Stein, *The Balfour Declaration*, p. 533 ff. Cf. also K. J. Herrmann, "Political Response to the Balfour Declaration in Imperial Germany," in *Middle East Journal,* XIX, 3, Summer 1965, pp. 303-320.

39. Cf. George-Samne, *La Syrie*, Paris, Bossard, 1920, a pro-French work, oriented along this line. After pages that reveal a great deal of perception, chapter XV, "Judaisme et Sionisme" (p. 396 ff.), concludes by proposing to the Zionists Jew-

ish autonomy within a Syrian confederation "under the temporary shield" of Syria's great, "loyal and disinterested" friend — France (p. 426).

40. *Trial and Error*, edition mentioned above, p. 192, for example.

41. *Ibid.*, p. 190.

42. The extent of the Arab contribution (Faisal's troops, hostility of Arab public opinion toward the Porte) has been much debated. It is reasonable to believe that although it was not unimportant, it was not decisive either.

43. Cf. the article by P. A. Alsberg, "The Arab question in the diplomacy of the Zionist Executive prior to the First World War" (in Hebrew), in *Shivat Tzion*, 4, 1956-1957, pp. 161-209.

44. In a very remarkable way, he let Herzl know in June 1896 that "the Turkish Empire does not belong to me, but rather to the Turkish people. I cannot distribute one piece of it. Let the Jews save their billions! When my Empire is divided up, they will be able to have Palestine for nothing. But what is divided up will be only our cadaver. I will not allow a vivisection." (R. Patai, ed.), *The Complete Diaries of Theodor Herzl*, New York, 1960, I, p. 378, quoted from Neville Mandel, article mentioned below (p. 23, n. 45), p. 87.

45. Cf. A. Chouraqui, *A Man Alone*, p. 183 ff.; Joan Haslip, *Le sultan, la tragedie d'Abdul Hamid*, French translation, Paris, Hachette, 1960, p. 226.

46. N. Mandel article referred to in the following note, p. 87.

47. Neville Mandel, "Turks, Arabs and Jewish Immigration into Palestine, 1882-1914," in *St. Antony's Papers*, No. 17 (*Middle Eastern Affairs*, No. 4), London, Oxford University Press, 1965, pp. 77-108.

48. N. Mandel, *ibid.*, p. 104 f.; M. Perlmann, "Chapters of Arab-Jewish Diplomacy 1918-1922" (in *Jewish Social Studies*, New York, vol. VI, No. 2, April 1944, pp. 123-154), p. 127.

49. N. Mandel, *ibid.,* p. 106.

50. For example, already the Jewish American justice Mayer Sulzberger, who around 1917 showed the contradiction between elementary principles of democracy and a Zionist project that made the fate of the Palestinians depend on people from the outside (referred to by Lenczowski in the work already mentioned, p. 375). Even more remarkable, and more concrete in its perceptiveness, is the letter from Jacques Bigard, secretary of the Universal Israelite Alliance, to Joseph Nehama, director of the Alliance in Salonica, dated May 3, 1918 (text in A. Chouraqui, *L'Alliance israelite universelle et la Renaissance juive contemporaine,* Paris, P.U.F., 1965, pp. 470-472).

51. Cf. the eloquent appraisal from someone who at that time was only a young American Zionist socialist activist in a letter from Palestine, where she had just arrived, to her brother-in-law, on August 24, 1921: "If we dig in here, England will come to our aid . . . It is not the Arabs whom the English will pick to have colonize Palestine, it is we." (in Marie Syrkin, *Golda Meir,* French translation, Paris, Gallimard, 1966, p. 63).

52. Elizabeth Monroe, *Britain's Moment in the Middle East,* 1914-1956, London, Chatto and Windus, 1963, p. 39; cf. G. Antonius, *Arab Awakening,* p. 246 f.

53. Weizmann, *Trial and Error,* p. 188.

54. Andre Chouraqui, *Theodore Herzl,* p. 256.

55. I was convinced by M. Perlmann's article, *Chapters of Arab-Jewish Diplomacy,* referred to above. It is quite true that G. Antonius has sought to minimize Faisal's concessions and to excuse them (*Arab Awakening,* p. 285 f.). But he publishes the text of the Weizmann-Faisal agreement with its dangerous vagueness on the status of Palestine, whose boundaries had to be fixed with the Arab state (pp. 437-439). I believe Sylvia G. Haim is overly harsh toward him in "*The Arab Awakening*: a Source for the Historian?" (in *Die Welt des Islams,* n.s., vol. II, Leiden-Koln, 1953, pp. 237-250). Antonius is a historian who is politically involved. Would to heaven all politically involved historians had kept things as well in proportion and been as objective as he!

56. This is certainly what justified Faisal's attitude in his own eyes. Cf. Weizmann, *Trial and Error*, p. 236ff; Antonius, *Arab Awakening*, p. 280 ff; Perlmann, *Chapters*, p. 130ff; A. Giannini, *L'ultima fase della questione orientale, 1913-1932*, Roma, Istituto per l'Oriente, 1933, p. 278ff; E. Rossi, *Documenti sull'origine e gli sviluppi della questione araba, 1875-1944*, Roma, Istituto per l'Oriente, 1944, p. 72ff.

57. Weizmann, *ibid.*, p. 245.

58. *Ibid.*, p. 247.

59. Antonius, *Arab Awakening*, p. 437ff; Rossi, *Documenti. . .*, p. 72ff; Weizmann, *ibid.*, p. 247 lessens the bite a little.

60. *Ibid.*, p. 247.

61. Rossi, *Documenti . . .*, p. 113ff; A. Giannini, *Documenti per la storia della pace orientale, 1915-1932*, Roma, Istituto per l'Oriente, 1933, p. 98ff. The Balfour Declaration was already ratified by the Treaty of Sevres with Turkey (August 10, 1920) in article 95 (Giannini, *Documenti. . .*, p. 44f).

62. Alexandre Bein, *Introduction au Sionisme*, Jerusalem, Rubin Mass, 1946 (*Sionisme, les faits et les idees:* Publications of the Youth Department of the World Zionist Organization), p. 105.

63. Brought out very well in Nathan Weinstock's interesting article *Israel, le sionisme et la lutte des classes*, in *Partisans*, No. 18, Dec. 1964, Jan. 1965, pp. 57-63 and No. 20, April-May 1965, pp. 20-32.

64. Bein, *Introduction au Sionisme*, p. 139.

65. Arthur Ruppin, *Les Juifs dans le monde moderne*, French translation, Paris, Payot, 1934, pp. 380-382.

66. Cf. A. Ruppin, *ibid.*, p. 380 f.; T. R. Feiwel, *L'Anglais, le Juif et l'Arabe en Palestine*, French translation, Paris, Ed. de France, 1939, p. 122 ff. It appears in English in *The Israel-Arab reader*, ed. by Walter Laqueur, New York, Bantam, 1969, p. 45.

67. Weizmann, *Trial and Error*, p. 291.

68. W. Stein, in *Vallentine's Jewish Encyclopaedia*, ed. by A.M. Hyamson and A.M. Silberman, London, Shapiro, Vallentine and Co., 1938, p. 552 b.

69. Weizmann, *Trial and Error*, p. 340. The present glorification of this individual in Israel is disturbing. In 1953 I quoted (from L. Dennens, *Where the Ghetto Ends*, New York, A.H. King, 1934, p. 233) the hymn sung by fashionable Jewish-Polish youth parading in brown uniforms and throwing rocks through the office windows of left-wing newspapers: "Germany for Hitler! — Italy for Mussolini! — Palestine for us! — Long Live Jabotinsky!" Judah L. Magnes bitterly wrote the following in 1946 regarding Jabotinsky's (premature) plans: "He found a big audience among the Poles, the Poles who are now carrying out pogroms. They wanted to get rid of the Jews in Poland and consequently accepted his evacuation plan" (in *Towards Union in Palestine*, Jerusalem, Ihud Association, 1947, p. 17). The Revisionist movement in fact received active support from the Polish right until around 1938.

70. N. Mandel, *Turks, Arabs and Jewish Immigration . . .*, p. 95 f.

71. E. Rossi, *Documenti . . .*, p. 114.

72. Robert Abdo Ghanem, *Les elements de formation d'un Etat juif en Palestine*, Beirut, Printing and Publishing Association, 1946 (Law department of the University of Lyon, French School of Law in Beirut). The date the thesis was defended is April 16, 1946.

73. A particularly revealing document is the work by the spokeswoman for the Stern group, Gueoula Cohen, *Souvenirs d'une jeune fille violente*, French text adapted by M. Politi, Paris, Gallimard, 1964 ("L'Air du temps," 197), a monument of semi-demented nationalist hysteria. Not for one instant does the idea even faintly occur to her that the Arabs in whose midst she operates and whose language, being a Yemenite, she speaks might have something to say about the fate of "her country."

74. According to Michael Bar Zohar, *Ben Gurion, the Armed*

Prophet, Englewood Cliffs, N. J., 1968, p. 68. Cf. the Stern-
ist Gueoula Cohen: [Great Britain formerly] "was all smiles
and pointed out the enemy for us to combat: Nazi Germany.
Already in 1940, the visionary Stern had been able to detect
clearly the double-dealing behind the smile, and had announced
who the real enemy to be defeated was: Great Britain" (*Souvenirs d'une jeune fille violente,* p. 127 f.); "every power in-
terested in seeing British imperialism liquidated [must be con-
sidered] a natural ally" (p. 289).

75. Martin Buber, "The Bi-National Approach to Zionism"
(in *Towards Union in Palestine, Essays on Zionism and Jew-
ish-Arab Cooperation,* ed. by M. Buber, J.L. Magnes, E. Simon,
Jerusalem, Ihud Association, 1947, pp. 7-13), p. 11.

76. Judah L. Magnes, "A Solution through Force?" (in the same
collection, pp. 14-21). Magnes, a man of admirable conscience,
was disheartened to see his ideas defeated and fled the young
State of Israel to die in the United States.

77. In G. Lenczowski, *The Middle East . . .,* p. 553, n. 9.
But on the other hand, an American congressman coming
out of a meeting with Roosevelt stated: "I feel that the President will be the new Moses who will lead the children of Israel
out of the desert" (*Palestine Post,* March 6, 1944).

78. G. Lenczowski, *ibid.,* p. 396.

79. See, for example, the disclosures made by Pvt. Clifford A.,
a soldier in the service of His Majesty, to J. F. Rolland in *Ce
Soir,* April 10, 1947. On the confusion of English responsibilities at all levels and what it was that came to impel the English
soldiers on the spot to determine that a pro-Arab policy held
sway in London, cf. the probing account by J. and D. Kimche,
Both Sides of the Hill, Britain and the Palestine War, London,
Secker and Warburg, 1960, p. 35 ff.

80. J. and D. Kimche, *ibid.,* p. 94.

81. E. Monroe, *Britain's Moment . . .,* p. 169. Cf. J. and D.
Kimche, *Both Sides . . .,* p. 86.

82. Related by the head of the Irgun, Menachem Begin, *The
Revolt, Story of the Irgun,* Tel Aviv, 1951, p. 348 ff. Com-

pare J. and D. Kimche, *Both Sides* . . ., pp. 82, 113. Case of intervention in favor of the Jews, *ibid.*, pp. 85, 94.

83. Cf. E. Monroe, *Britain's Moment*, p. 163ff; J. and D. Kimche, *Both Sides of the Hill*, p. 21ff.

84. *Ibid.*, p. 78 f.

85. On the "great plan" of D. Ben Gurion to reach a tacit agreement with King Abdallah on a partition of Palestine under the aegis of Great Britain (which had become more understanding), a plan that the actors in the drama did not know about and which explains many of the puzzling twists and turns in the struggle, cf. the posthumous book written in prison by Israel Beer, *Bitachon Yisrael* (The Security of Israel), Tel Aviv, ed. Amikam, 1966, particularly chapter II (pp. 115-215). It is to be hoped that this important book by a man with access to first-hand information will be translated into a European language.

86. J. and D. Kimche, *Both Sides* . . ., pp. 45, 64.

87. Meticulous account by A.-M. Goichon, "Les responsabilites de la guerre de Palestine" (in *Correspondance d'Orient, Etudes*, Brussels, vol. VII, 1965, pp. 3-28). Cf. Glubb Pasha, *Soldat avec les Arabes*, French translation, Paris, Plon, 1958, p. 43 and especially J. and D. Kimche, *Both Sides* . . ., and I. Beer, *Bitachon* . . ., chap. II.

88. Cf. Glubb Pasha, *ibid.*, p. 73 f. But he exaggerates the Israeli figures (65,000 men). It would seem that more confidence can be placed in the figures given by J. and D. Kimche, *Both Sides* . . ., p. 160 f.

89. *Ibid.*, p. 223; compare pp. 233, 243.

90. Cf. Lenczowski, *The Middle East* . . ., p. 398 ff. and for example J. and D. Kimche, *Both Sides* . . ., p. 218 ff.

91. Lenczowski, *ibid.*, p. 398, n. 39; J. and D. Kimche, p. 223. The Egyptians got around the difficulty by pillaging British storehouses in the Suez canal zone. The volunteers of the Liberation Army were supplied particularly badly (J. and D. Kimche, p. 81 f.).

92. One can read about all this in the informative recollections of Colonel B. Kagan, *Combat secret pour Israel*, Paris, Hachette, 1963, with a preface by J. Larteguy which could have been dispensed with and which simply contradicts the author (on Czech aid). Compare J. and D. Kimche, *Both Sides. . .*, p. 204 ff.

93. Cf. Walter Schwarz, *The Arabs in Israel*, London, Faber and Faber, 1959, a book whose tone is remarkably fair; written by a British journalist who spent eighteen months in Israel, traveling with his wife by donkey in the Arab sectors.

94. Only a racist or mystical concept of "Jewishness" (with the latter being common among left-wing Europeans) can explain shock that conditions that everywhere else bring about a state with a racist mentality (an ethnic cleavage coinciding with a social cleavage) are also at work in the case of Jews.

95. The history of these efforts has been especially traced by the militant Orientalist Aharon Cohen of Mapam. Cf. finally his huge book *Israel and the Arab World*, New York, Funk & Wagnalls, 1970, 576 pp. On one of these efforts, in 1936, where the Arabs were ready to accept a high annual quota of Jewish immigrants in terms of prevailing criteria, cf. the documents edited by *Ner*, vol. 12, No. 9-10, July-August 1961, p. 24 ff. In 1943, yet another Arab offer of a binational state with equality for both peoples was spurned by the Jewish Agency; cf. Nathan Chofshi, in *Towards Union in Palestine*, p. 39.

96. Marie Syrkin, *Golda Meir*, French translation, Paris, Gallimard, 1966, p. 133.

97. Including certain Arabs before the spread of nationalist ideology and anti-Zionist theoretical arguments among the masses did away with these kinds of attitudes. Cf. N. Mandel, *Turks, Arabs and Jewish Immigration*, p. 89.

98. Cf. the texts I collected in *Voies Nouvelles*, No. 9 (June 1959), pp. 26-31.

99. I read the following in a very left-wing Zionist publication: "It is the attitude toward Israel, the historical homeland of the Jewish people, that acts as a kind of barometer for many re-

gimes, for all governments . . . One is not progressive, but [and, it might be added, *also*] anti-Israeli . . . This anti-Israelism is not a blemish in this or that blue sky: it is an absolute evil worthy only of a reactionary mind" (*Cahiers Bernard Lazare*, No. 21-22, Nov.-Dec. 1963, p. 25). A senseless attempt to confer a sacred character on a state on the basis of nothing more than the Jewishness of the majority of its citizens! If this is not racism, what is?

100. Letter from Engels to Kautsky, September 12, 1882, quoted and expanded upon by Lenin, *The Right of Nations to Self-Determination*, New York, International Publishers, p. 114.

101. I can foresee the outcry against such a statement, going as it does against the various neo-Marxist philosophies and ideologies built up over the past hundred years out of disparate materials, drawn from the ideas, arguments, feelings, etc., of Marx and Engels, and made into a system in contexts that were quite different. Therefore I will make myself very clear. It seems to me undeniable that, first, man's biological condition which has scarcely changed since the Paleolithic age, and second, the most general characteristics of every possible society, and finally third, the very general characteristics that, while doubtless not eternal, nonetheless transcend the various particular social formations existing since the beginnings of human history (or at least since the neolithic revolution) have together conditioned a body of very general and very lasting psychological traits that characterize historical man. He will no doubt change even so far as these points are concerned. But the experiment of half a century of Soviet society with no private property in the means of production shows that he resists the effort to abolish these psychological traits. This goes against the ideology of Marx himself. It conforms to his sociology, or rather to a sociology based on the principles he defined. Furthermore, occasionally Marx himself spoke of human nature; cf. references cited by S. F. Bloom, *The World of Nations*, New York, Columbia University Press, 1941, p. 2, and in *Journal of the History of Ideas*, 7, 1946, p. 119.

102. *In its early stages*, the Soviet Union offered the Jews three possibilities to choose from: assimilation, cultural autonomy for the Yiddish-speaking Jewish "nationality" in areas

it already occupied, or an autonomous Jewish region. The way the policy toward nationalities in the Stalin era resulted in practice in thwarting assimilation; the way the war resulted in the authorities capitulating to the persistent anti-Semitism of the masses that suddenly surfaced openly in full force; and the way the persistence of Jewish national feelings that was caused by this whole policy and discovered with the arrival of the first Israeli ambassador prompted Stalin to unleash his clearly anti-Semitic measures — all this is part of a long history that cannot be gone into here and that has nothing to do with any anti-Semitic "essence" of Marxism, as R. Misrahi believes. But the Birobidjan failure, which Zionists feed upon, is not fraught with significance. It proves that in the first period, the other solutions offered to the Soviet Jews did not meet with too many objections from them, and that the idea of Birobidjan had been conceived without investing it with very attractive qualities. This only got worse as time went on.

103. A dynamic that is described well by Michael Ionides, *Divide and Lose, the Arab Revolt of 1955-1958*, London, Geoffrey Bliss, 1960, with regard to a later period, but a good part of which is valid for the period 1920-1948.

104. Cf. for example the good account by Paul Sebag, *La Tunisie, essai de monographie*, Paris, Ed. Sociales, 1951, p. 36 f.

105. About these confiscations, cf. the honest and well documented account by W. Schwarz, *The Arabs in Israel*, p. 96 ff.; more details in Don Peretz, *Israel and the Palestine Arabs*, Washington, The Middle East Institute, 1958; the laws referred to can be found conveniently translated in *Fundamental Laws of the State of Israel*, Joseph Badi editor, New York, Twayne Publishers, 1961. The collection of the review *Ner*, edited in Israel by the courageous little group Ihud, contains many documents and protests on this theme. From Schwarz let us quote the letter from its Central Committee (among whom were Martin Buber, E. Simon, S. Shereshevsky and the president of the Legal Committee of the Knesset) protesting "the lands consolidation law, which really means theft of lands for some people, for people who are inhabitants of the state. They are farmers just like you. They are citizens of Israel just like you. There is only one difference between them and

you: they are Arabs and you are Jews" (*Ner*, April 1953; Schwarz, p. 102). See also the article by S. Shereshevsky, "Against the Agricultural Lands Consolidation Law" in *Ner*, vol. XII, No. 5-6, March-April 1961, pp. I-V. Regarding this new law that "the Arabs with reason will regard as racist legislation designed to 'Judaize Galilee' by expelling the Arab population," the author recalls the March 10, 1953, land consolidation law mentioned above. Under the pretext of "vital needs of development, settlement and security . . ., innumerable acts of injustice were perpetrated against those whose lands were 'consolidated' in this way, including fixed low prices, compensation that in many cases has not been paid to this day, the mean and insulting attitude toward the Arab owners whose lands, and whose ancestors' lands, were confiscated, 'merely because the Jewish *kibbutzim* and *moshavim* want to add to their possessions,' as [the socialist newspaper] *Haaretz* puts it." It can be seen that a communal life style by no means renders the desire to appropriate (collectively, of course) the wealth of others impossible.

106. *Statistical Handbook of Middle Eastern Countries*, Jerusalem, Jewish Agency for Palestine, Economic Research Institute, 1944, p. 10; J. Klatzmann, *Les enseignements de l'experience israelienne*, Paris, P.U.F., 1963 (Collection "Tiers-Monde"), p. 285.

107. A guarded estimate that W. Schwarz (p. 99) arrives at after discussing the facts at hand.

108. Let us note, moreover, that there are two sides to this fact. The small Arab tenants on lands sold by big landholders, who were chased off these lands by virtue of the sacrosanct rule providing for exclusively Jewish labor, found no consolation in the thought that strictly egalitarian relations were going to (sometimes) prevail on this property.

109. This is a very complicated question. See A.-M. Goichon's articles in the July and August-September 1964 issues of *Esprit*. The most common motive for the flight of the Arabs appears to have been quite simply panic at the prospect of war, as in Spain in 1939 or France in 1940. In any case, there can be no doubt that the Israeli Oradour, the deliberate massacre the night of April 9-10, 1948, by the *Irgun* of 254 men, women, and children in the Arab village of Dir Yassin, had

a dramatic effect on this flight. The only person to deny that it was a massacre was the head of the Irgun, Menachem Begin, who nonetheless bragged about the effect of the "lies" about Dir Yassin: "All the Jewish forces proceeded to advance through Haifa like a knife through butter. The Arabs began fleeing in panic, shouting Dir Yassin!" (*The Revolt, Story of the Irgun*, p. 165, corroborated by J. and D. Kimche, *Both Sides . . .*, p. 124; cf. M. Bar Zohar, *Ben Gurion, the Armed Prophet*, pp. 107-108). Many Jews like the supreme leader D. Ben Gurion hoped, very logically, that the greatest possible number of Arabs would leave. His hagiographer, Michael Bar-Zohar, candidly writes: "The fewer [Arabs] there were living within the frontiers of the new Jewish state, the better he would like it. . . . (While this might be called racialism, the whole Zionist movement actually was based on the principle of a purely Jewish community in Palestine. When various Zionist institutions appealed to the Arabs not to leave the Jewish State but to become an integral part of it, they were being hypocritical to some extent)." (*Ben Gurion*, p. 103f.) It could not have been said any better!

110. Walter Schwarz, *The Arabs in Israel*, London, Faber and Faber, 1959.

111. Alex Weingrod, Israel, *Group Relations in a New Society*, London, Pall Mall Press, 1965 (Institute of Race Relations), p. 70f.

112. The annexation of the non-Israeli West Bank by the Hashemite Kingdom of Transjordan, placing the Palestine Arabs under a sovereignty they did not want, was a consequence (one Israel hoped for) of proclaiming the Jewish state and of the 1948 war.

113. Rene Maunier, *Sociologie coloniale, (I), Introduction a l'etude du contact des races*, Paris, Domat-Montchrestien, 1932, p. 37; cf. p. 21. Let us note, moreover, that for a long time, as we could see in the texts mentioned above, the Zionists readily and without being self-conscious used the terms "colonial" and "colonies" in the names of their institutions and in their documents, whether official or not, etc., to describe their plans.

114. Cf. the article in which I developed this line of argument,

"Israel, une lutte de liberation nationale?" (in *Partisans*, No. 21, June-August 1965, pp. 34-40).

115. A key difference in comparison to European anti-Semitism, where the anti-Semitic myth is based either on accusations lacking even a shadow of a foundation or on the results of a situation that was *imposed* on the Jews. The myth, by alone giving them meaning, helped organize imaginary grievances, or when there was some truth to them, grievances that were not the product of the free will of the Jewish groups but of the social situation in which they had been forcibly placed (the practice of usury, for example). Arab anti-Zionism, in contrast, essentially develops out of a very real grievance (even if some may wish to excuse or justify it), out of a situation created *by* the free will of powerful Jewish groups proclaiming that they represent Jews as a whole. Only this real grievance gives some meaning to the anti-Semitic myths occasionally put forward to "explain" it, and without it these myths lose any power they might have.

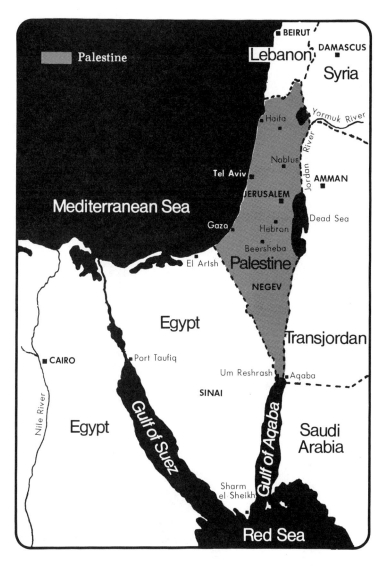

Palestine Under the British Mandate

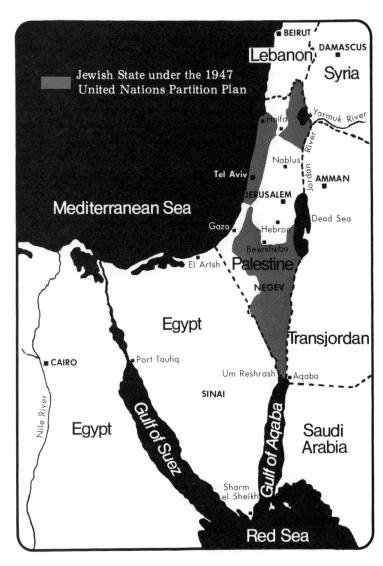

Jewish State under the 1947
United Nations Partition Plan

BEIRUT
DAMASCUS
Lebanon
Syria
Yarmuk River
Haifa
Nablus
Tel Aviv
AMMAN
JERUSALEM
Mediterranean Sea
Dead Sea
Gaza
Hebron
Beersheba
El Arish
Palestine
NEGEV
Egypt
Transjordan
CAIRO
Port Taufiq
Um Reshrash
Aqaba
SINAI
Nile River
Egypt
Gulf of Suez
Saudi
Arabia
Gulf of Aqaba
Sharm
el Sheikh
Red Sea

1947 United Nations Partition Plan

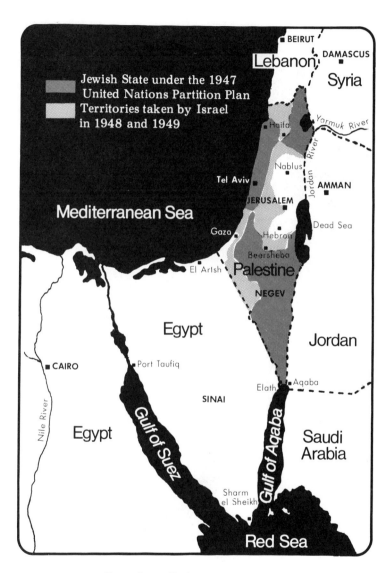

Results of the 1948 War

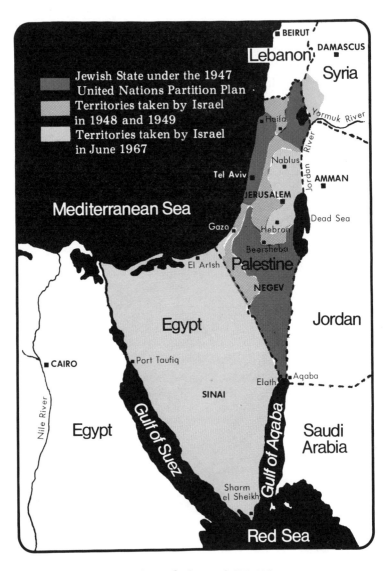

Jewish State under the 1947
United Nations Partition Plan
Territories taken by Israel
in 1948 and 1949
Territories taken by Israel
in June 1967

BEIRUT
DAMASCUS
Lebanon
Syria
Yarmuk River
Haifa
Jordan River
Nablus
Tel Aviv
AMMAN
JERUSALEM
Mediterranean Sea
Dead Sea
Gaza
Hebron
Beersheba
El Arish
Palestine
NEGEV
Egypt
Jordan
CAIRO
Port Taufiq
Elath
Aqaba
SINAI
Nile River
Egypt
Gulf of Suez
Gulf of Aqaba
Saudi
Arabia
Sharm
el Sheikh
Red Sea

Results of the 1967 War

Further reading

THE JEWISH QUESTION

A MARXIST INTERPRETATION

by Abram Leon

Traces the historical rationalizations of anti-Semitism to the position of Jews as a "people-class" of merchants and moneylenders in the centuries leading up to the domination of industrial capitalism. Leon explains how in times of social crisis renewed Jew-hatred is incited by the capitalists to mobilize reactionary forces against the labor movement and disorient the middle classes and layers of working people about the true source of their impoverishment. $17.95

PALESTINE AND THE ARABS' FIGHT FOR LIBERATION

by Fred Feldman and Georges Sayad

An overview of the Palestinian struggle from World War I to the beginning of the intifada in 1987. Booklet. $4.00

SOCIALISTS AND THE FIGHT AGAINST ANTI-SEMITISM

AN ANSWER TO THE B'NAI B'RITH ANTI-DEFAMATION LEAGUE

by Peter Seidman

The real record of the fight to open Washington's doors to refugees from Hitler's terror. Booklet. $3.00

FASCISM: WHAT IT IS AND HOW TO FIGHT IT

by Leon Trotsky

Fascism, Trotsky explains, has been able to conquer in those countries where social democratic or Stalinist parties blocked the proletariat from utilizing a revolutionary situation to remove the capitalists from power. Booklet. $3.00

ON THE JEWISH QUESTION

by Leon Trotsky

"Never was it so clear as it is today that the salvation of the Jewish people is bound up inseparably with the overthrow of the capitalist system."—Leon Trotsky, 1940. Booklet. $3.00

WRITE FOR A CATALOG. SEE FRONT OF BOOK FOR ADDRESSES.

Also from Pathfinder

NELSON MANDELA SPEAKS
Forging a Democratic, Nonracial South Africa

Tells the story of the struggles that are opening a deep-going transformation of political, economic, and social conditions in the former land of apartheid. $18.95

TO SPEAK THE TRUTH
Why Washington's 'Cold War' Against Cuba Doesn't End
BY FIDEL CASTRO AND CHE GUEVARA

Why the U.S. government is determined to destroy the example set by the socialist revolution in Cuba and why its effort will fail. Introduction by Mary-Alice Waters. $16.95

TO SEE THE DAWN
Baku, 1920—First Congress of the Peoples of the East

How can peasants and workers in the colonial world achieve freedom from imperialist exploitation? How can working people overcome divisions incited by their national ruling classes and act together for their common class interests? These questions were addressed by 2,000 delegates to the 1920 Congress of the Peoples of the East. Complete proceedings. $19.95

MALCOLM X ON AFRO-AMERICAN HISTORY

Recounts the hidden history of the labor of people of African origin and their achievements—related to preparation for struggles today. $8.95

THE HISTORY OF THE RUSSIAN REVOLUTION
BY LEON TROTSKY

The social, economic, and political dynamics of the first victorious socialist revolution, as told by one of its principal leaders. Unique in modern literature. Unabridged edition, 3 vols. in one. 1,358 pp. $35.95

THE CHANGING FACE OF U.S. POLITICS
Working-Class Politics and the Trade Unions
BY JACK BARNES

A handbook for the generations of workers coming into the factories, mines, and mills—workers who will react to the uncertain life, ceaseless turmoil, and brutality that will accompany the arrival of the twenty-first century. It shows why only the working class can lead humanity out of the social crisis endemic to capitalism in its decline. And how millions of workers, as political resistance grows, will revolutionize themselves, their unions, and all of society. New, expanded edition. $19.95

COSMETICS, FASHIONS, AND THE EXPLOITATION OF WOMEN
BY JOSEPH HANSEN, EVELYN REED, AND MARY-ALICE WATERS

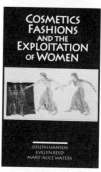

How big business uses women's second-class status to generate profits for a few and perpetuate the oppression of the female sex and the exploitation of working people. $12.95

THE COMMUNIST MANIFESTO
BY KARL MARX AND FREDERICK ENGELS

Founding document, written in 1847, of the modern working-class movement. Explains how capitalism arose as a specific stage in the economic development of class society and how it will be superseded through revolutionary action on a world scale by the working class. Booklet. $2.50

UNDERSTANDING HISTORY
Marxist Essays
BY GEORGE NOVACK

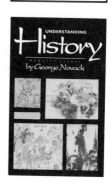

How did capitalism arise? Why has this exploitative system exhausted its potential? Why is revolutionary change in society and political relations, not just gradual social development, fundamental to human progress? $15.95

WRITE FOR A FREE CATALOG. SEE ADDRESSES AT FRONT OF BOOK.

New International

A MAGAZINE OF MARXIST POLITICS AND THEORY

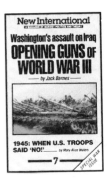

DISTRIBUTED BY PATHFINDER